Dictionary of Surnames

The Wordsworth

Dictionary of Surnames

–

*Terry Freedman and
Iseabail Macleod*

Wordsworth Reference

This edition published 1997 by Wordsworth Editions Ltd
Cumberland House, Crib Street, Ware, Hertfordshire SG12 9ET

ISBN 1 85326 380 X

Typeset by Antony Gray
Printed and bound in Great Britain by
Mackays of Chatham plc, Chatham, Kent

INTRODUCTION

Out of the vast range of British surnames, this dictionary offers a selection of about 3000 entries, with some of their variant forms. To the mass of common names, we have added a number of unusual ones, and also examples such as **Thoroughgood** and **Charlesworth,** whose origins are not as straightforward as they seem. There is a sprinkling of names, like **Rollo**, which are not as exotic as they look. The names are classified in four categories: personal names, like **Thomas**, occupational names, such as **Wainwright,** nicknames, such as **Dainty**, and finally place names. The last group is really composed of two types: those like **Minshull** which are names of actual towns, villages and other places and, on the other hand, those like **Hill** which refer to features of the landscape.

Surnames, which developed into a system in the Middle Ages, reflect the common history and culture of the families bearing them, though, except in the case of a few aristocratic dynasties, they do not necessarily reflect an individual's family history. This is because in the past a man sometimes adopted the surname of his master and members of the same family sometimes changed or spelt their surname in a variety of ways as they fancied. A clerk or scribe could easily record a name incorrectly. Those surnames formed from personal names reveal which particular Christian names were current in the Middle Ages. Names like **Bunyan** show that personal defects provided nicknames which became permanent names. The occupational category contains reminders of once-important craftsmen whose trades no longer exist, such as **Habersham**, referring to a maker of chain mail. Place names are frequently evidence of the migrations from the countryside to the fast-growing towns from the Middle Ages onwards. It must often have been convenient to refer to a newcomer to the city by his birthplace and, in time, the name of a person's obscure little village, or even his country of origin, became his or her official family name.

Many Scottish and Irish surnames derive from Gaelic and begin with **Mac** meaning 'son of', often reduced to **Mc** or even **M'**. Such names are usually written as one word, like **MacDonald** or **Macdonald**, and there is argument as to whether the second element should begin with a capital letter or not. Unanglicized Irish names, however, are written as two words, with a capital letter to start the second element, eg **Mac Lachlainn.** We have listed all these names, whether spelt **Mac** or **Mc,** under **Mac.** Other Irish names begin with **O,** meaning 'grandson, descendant of', as in **O Ryan.** A further group begins with **Fitz–,** from Old French meaning 'son of', a relic of the strong influence of the Normans on medieval Ireland.

Northern Irish names are an interesting mix of Irish and Scottish elements because the connections between the two places remained close throughout the centuries and Gaelic-speaking peoples of these areas formed a common culture throughout the Middle Ages. In the 17th century, many Lowland Scots and English were settled in N Ireland, by the crown under a policy known as the Plantations, thus introducing new surnames.

It was only around 1600 that hereditary surnames slowly began to be used in Wales. Many of the most common are personal names from English, such as **Evan,** the Welsh form of **John,** or **Davis,** from **David.** Others such as **Howell** are from Old Welsh names. Both types have changed into different forms with the addition of 'ap' meaning 'son of', as in **Powell,** formed from 'ap' + '**Howell**', or **Bevan,** from 'ap' + '**Evan**' (because the 'p' of 'ap' was originally 'b'). The most common English equivalents of these elements meaning 'son of' or 'descendant of' are 'son', as in **Johnson,** or 's' as in **Adams.**

Other Forms
Since surnames appear in various forms we have tried to include the commonest alternatives, listing them as far as possible in order of frequency. In cases where this is not obvious, the alternative forms have been listed alphabetically, eg

Lee
Other forms: **Attlee, Lay(e), Lea, Lees, Leigh, Ley, Lye**
These forms are given their own entries eg
Attlee other form of **Lee**

Pronunciation

This is occasionally indicated where it may present a problem. The stressed syllable is marked by bold type, eg

Lamont [**la**-mont]

It should be noted that some of the pronunciation guides to Scottish, Welsh and Irish names are only approximate.

–kh = the last sound in Scottish 'loch' or Welsh 'bach'

Languages

The following languages are referred to in explanations of the names:

English

Old English – from its Anglo-Saxon origins up to the 11th century

Middle English – from the 12th to the 15th century

Scots – the language of Lowland Scotland, descended from N Old English

Older Scots – up to 1700

Old Norse – the ancestor of the Scandinavian languages, once widely spoken in the British Isles

Celtic – a group of languages subdivided into two broad groups: the first consists of Welsh, Breton and Cornish, the other of Irish, Scottish and Manx Gaelic

Old Welsh – the ancestor of modern Welsh (sometimes called Brittonic or British), once widely spoken over the British mainland

Irish Gaelic – the Celtic language of Ireland

Scottish Gaelic – the Celtic language of Scotland

Acknowledgements

We would like to thank the many people who have given us advice, in particular Robert Mullally for his expert help on Irish names, Celia Yates for providing examples of unusual surnames and David Freedman for his reading of the manuscript and his helpful suggestions.

A

Abbot other form of **Abbott**

Abbott
Other form: **Abbot**
English – occupational; from Middle English meaning 'abbot', usually referring to someone employed by an abbot.

Abel
English – personal name; from the first name, itself from Hebrew meaning 'breath'.

Abercrombie
Other form: **Abercromby**
Scottish – place name; from the village in Fife, the name deriving from Celtic meaning 'mouth of the winding stream'.

Abernethy
Scottish – place name; from the town near Perth, the name deriving from Celtic meaning 'rivermouth' + an old river name of doubtful origin.

Ablewhite other form of **Applethwaite**

Abraham
Other forms: **Abram**, **Abrahamson**
English – personal name; from the first name, itself from Hebrew meaning 'father of the multitude'.

Acheson Scottish form of **Adams**

Ackroyd
English – place name; from Northern Middle English meaning 'oak' + 'clearing'.

A'Court other form of **Court**

Adair
Scottish – personal name; probably from a variant form of **Edgar**; the name has been known in Galloway since medieval times.

Adams
Other forms: **Acheson**, **Adam**, **Adamson**, **Addison**, **Adie**, **Aiken**, **Aitken**, **Atkins**, **Atkinson**

English – personal name; from the first name **Adam**, itself from Hebrew meaning 'red'.

Affery other form of **Aubrey**

Agar other form of **Edgar**

Agate

English – place name; from Middle English meaning 'by a gate'.

Agnew

English and Scottish

1 place name; from Agneaux in France. The name, whose origin is unknown, probably took this form because of a popular misapprehension that it derived from French meaning 'lambs'

2 nickname; from Old French meaning 'lamb', referring to someone meek and mild, or pure.

Agutter

English – place name; from Middle English meaning 'at the gutter or water course'.

Ahearne other form of **Aherne**

Aherne

Other forms: **Ahern**, **Ahearne**, **Hearne**

Irish – personal name; anglicized form of Irish Gaelic **Ó hEachthighearna**, descendant of **Eachthighearna**, itself meaning 'horse' + 'master'.

Aiken other form of **Adams**

Ainsworth

English – place name; from a place near Manchester, the name deriving from the Old English name **Aegen** + 'enclosure'.

Aitken other form of **Adams**

Albee

Other form: **Alby**

English – place name; from places in Norfolk and Lincolnshire, the name deriving from the Old Norse name **Ali** + 'farm, settlement'. Edward Albee (1928–) is an American dramatist.

Alcott

Other form: **Aucutt**

English – place name; from Old English meaning 'old' + 'cottage'. Louisa May Alcott (1832–88) was an American novelist and author of the children's classic *Little Women*.

Aldridge

English – place name; from places in Staffordshire and Buckinghamshire, the name deriving from Old English meaning either 'dairy farm in the alders' or 'ridge of the alders'.

Alexander

Other forms: **Sander(s)**, **Sanderson**, **Saunders**

English – personal name; from the first name, itself from Latin, based on Greek meaning 'defend' + 'man warrior'.

Alford

English – place name; from a place in Somerset, the name deriving from an Old English name meaning 'old war' + 'ford'.

Algar other form of **Alger**

Alger

Other forms: **Algar**, **Elgar**

English – personal name; from a Middle English name **Alger**, itself deriving from several Germanic names, which mean either 'elf' or 'old' + 'spear'.

Allan

Other form: **Allen**

English – personal name; from the first name **Alan**, itself of uncertain origin. Woody Allen (1935–) is an American film actor and director. See also **Mac Allan.**

Allaun

English – place name; from Old French meaning 'at the lawn' or 'at the glade'.

Allen other form of **Allan**

Allenby

English – place name; from places in Cumberland, the name deriving from **Alan** + Old Norse meaning 'farm'.

Allinson other form of **Allison**

Allison

Scottish – personal name;

1 From the female name **Alice** or **Alison**.

2 Shortened form of **Allinson**, 'son of **Alan**'.

3 From the first name **Alister**, itself an anglicized form of **Alasdair**, Scottish Gaelic form of **Alexander.**

Alloway

Other form: **Halloway**

English – personal name; from the Old English name **Aethelwig**, itself meaning 'noble' + 'battle'.

Allsop

Other form: **Alsop**

English – place name; from the place in Derbyshire, the name deriving from an Old English personal name **Aelli** + 'valley'.

Almond

English – personal name; from an Old English name meaning 'noble' + 'protector'.

Alsop other form of **Allsop.**

Alton

English – place name; from places in many areas of England, the name deriving from different Old English sources. In Hampshire, Wiltshire and Dorset, the name derives from 'spring' + 'enclosure'. In the Midlands, the name derives from 'old' + 'enclosure' and in a few places, the first part is an Old English name, **Aelfa.**

Ambler

English – occupational; either from Norman-French of Germanic origin meaning 'enameller', or from Middle English meaning 'walker'. In the latter case, the term was used of the gait of a horse and may refer to a stableman's job.

Amery

Other forms: **Emery, Embury**

English – personal name; from the name **Amalric**, itself from Norman-French based on Germanic meaning 'bravery' + 'power'.

Ames other form of **Amis.**

Amis

Other forms: **Ames, Amos**

English – personal name; from the Old French name **Amis**, itself from Latin meaning 'friend'. Kingsley Amis (1922–95) was an English novelist famous for his first novel *Lucky Jim*; his son Martin Amis (1949–) is also a successful novelist.

Anderson other form of **Andrew**

Andress other form of **Andrew**

Andrew

Other forms: **Andrews**, **Anderson**, **Drew**, **Andress**, **Tandy**, **Dandy**

English – personal name; from the first name, itself from Greek meaning 'manly'.

Angus

Other form: **Innes**

Scottish – personal name/place name; either from the personal name, itself from Scottish Gaelic **Aonghus**, probably meaning 'one' + 'choice', or from the place name, the area north of the Tay, itself probably derived from the personal name, possibly in honour of an 8th-century Pictish king.

Ansell

English – personal name; from the Germanic name **Anselm** meaning 'god' + 'helmet, protection'.

Anstey

English – place name; from many places, the name deriving from Old English meaning 'one' + 'path', indicating a road that had a fork at both ends.

Antrobus

English – place name; from a place in Cheshire, the name deriving from an Old Norse name **Andrithi** + Old Norse meaning 'bush'.

Applethwaite

Other forms: **Ablewhite**, **Applewhite**

English – place name; from places in Cumbria, the name deriving from Old Norse meaning 'apple' + 'meadow'.

Apps

Other forms: **Aspey**, **Epps**

English – place name; from Middle English meaning 'aspen tree'.

Arbuthnot

Other form: **Arbuthnott**

Scottish – place name; from the Kincardineshire place name, deriving from Scottish Gaelic meaning 'rivermouth' + 'little virtue' (indicating a holy stream).

Archbold other form of **Archibald**

Archer

English – occupational; from Old French meaning 'bowman'. Jeffrey Archer (1940–) is a British author.

Archibald
Other form: **Archbold**
English and Scottish – personal name; from the first name, itself from Germanic meaning 'noble' + 'bold'.

Arden
English – place name; from the Forest of Arden in Warwickshire, or from a place in Yorkshire, the name deriving from Celtic meaning 'high'.

Arkwright
Other form: **Hattrick**
English – occupational; from Middle English meaning 'ark, chest' + 'craftsman', referring to a maker of chests. Sir Richard Arkwright (1732–92) was an English inventor and industrialist who invented the water-powered spinning frame.

Arlott
English – nickname; from Middle English meaning 'rascal, vagabond'.

Armitage
English – place name; from Middle English meaning 'hermitage'.

Armstrong
N English and S Scottish – nickname; meaning 'strong-armed'. The name was well-known on both sides of the English-Scottish Border, but more especially on the Scottish side, where many of its bearers had legendary fame as Border reivers or freebooters, notably Armstrong of Gilnockie, executed by James V in 1529. Neil Armstrong (1930–), the American astronaut and first man on the moon, is of Scottish descent.

Arnason, Arnison other forms of Arnold

Arnold
English – Other forms: **Arnason, Arnison, Arnott**
1 personal name; from Norman-French of Germanic origin meaning 'eagle' + 'rule'.
2 place name; from places in Nottinghamshire and Yorkshire, the name deriving from Old English meaning 'eagle' + 'nook, hollow'. Matthew Arnold (1822–88) was an English poet and critic.

Arnot other form of Arnott

Arnott
Other form: **Arnot**
1 English – personal name; other form of **Arnold**.
2 Scottish – place name; from the place near Kinross, the name

possibly deriving from Scottish Gaelic meaning 'barley land'.

Arrowsmith

Other forms: **Harrismith**, **Harrowsmith**

English – occupational; from Old English meaning 'maker of arrows'.

Arthur

Other forms: **Arthus**, **Arthuys**

English – personal name; from the first name, itself of uncertain origin, first found in its Latin form **Artorius.**

Ashdown

English – place name; from the forest in Sussex, the name deriving from Old English meaning 'ash tree' + 'hill'. Paddy Ashdown (1941–) is an English Liberal Democrat politician.

Ashley

English – place name; from numerous places, the name deriving from Old English meaning 'ash' + 'wood'.

Ashwin

English – personal name; from Old English meaning 'spear' + 'friend'.

Aske

English – place name; from a place in Yorkshire, the name deriving from Old Norse meaning 'ash tree'.

Askew

Other forms: **Askey**, **Ayscough**

English – place name; from a place in Yorkshire, the name deriving from Old Norse meaning 'oak wood'.

Askwith other form of **Asquith**

Aslam, **Aslen**, other forms of **Haslam**

Aspey other form of **Apps**

Aspinall

English – place name; from a place in Lancashire, the name deriving from Old English meaning 'aspen' + 'stream'.

Asquith

Other form: **Askwith**

English – place name; from a place in Yorkshire, the name deriving from Old Norse meaning 'ash' + 'wood'. Herbert Henry Asquith, 1st Earl of Oxford and Asquith (1852–1928), was a British Liberal statesman who became prime minister in 1908.

Atkey other form of **Kay**

Atkins, Atkinson other forms of **Adams**

Attenborough
English – place name; from Middle English meaning 'at the manor house'. Two famous brothers are Sir Richard Attenborough (1923–), film director, and Sir David Attenborough (1926–), naturalist.

Attfield other form of **Field**

Attlee other form of **Lee**

Aubrey
Other forms: **Avery, Affery**
English – personal name; from a Middle English name **Aubri**, itself from Germanic meaning 'elf counsel'.

Aucutt other form of **Alcott**

Auld
Scottish – nickname; from Scots meaning 'old'.

Austen other form of **Austin**

Austin
Other form: **Austen**
English – personal name; from the Middle English name **Austin**, itself from the Latin name **Augustinus**, meaning 'venerable'. Jane Austen (1775–1817) was an English novelist.

Avery other form of **Aubrey**

Ayckbourn
English – place name; from Old Norse meaning 'oak' + 'stream'. Alan Ayckbourn (1939–) is an English playwright.

Ayer
Other forms: **Ayers, Eyre, Hayer, Heyer**
English – nickname; from Middle English meaning 'heir', referring to someone who would inherit a substantial fortune. Sir Alfred Jules Ayer (1910–89) was an English philosopher.

Ayscough other form of **Askew**

B

Babb

Other forms: **Babbitt, Babcock**

English – personal name; either from the medieval name **Babb**, a familiar form of **Barbara**, itself from Greek meaning 'foreign woman', or else from an Old English name **Babba.**

Bachelor

Other form: **Batchelor**

English – occupational; from Old French meaning 'young knight at arms'. (The term only later came to mean an unmarried man.)

Bacon

Other forms: **Baggott, Bagehot**

English

1 occupational; from Middle English meaning 'cured pork, ham', referring to a seller of ham and pork.

2 personal name; from a Germanic name **Baco**, itself from Germanic meaning 'to fight'. Francis Bacon, Viscount St Albans, (1561–1626) was an English philosopher and statesman. Francis Bacon (1909–94) was an Irish artist regarded as a major modern painter.

Bagehot other form of **Bacon**

Baggot other form of **Bacon**

Bagnall

Other forms: **Bagnell, Bagnold**

English – place name; from a place in Staffordshire, the name deriving from an Old English name **Badeca**, itself from Old English meaning 'battle' + 'nook, recess'.

Bagshaw

English – place name; from a place in Derbyshire, the name deriving from an Old English name **Bacga** + 'wood, copse'.

Bailey

Other forms: **Baily, Baillie** (mainly Scottish)

1 English and Scottish – occupational; from Middle English meaning 'official, steward', referring to someone who was an official in the royal service, keeper of a building, an agent or a factor.

2 English – place name; from Middle English meaning 'enclosure', referring originally to part of a castle, as in the case of the Old Bailey in London. In some cases, however, the name derives from Old English meaning 'berry' + 'wood, clearing', as in Bailey in Lancashire.

Bain

Other forms: **Baines, Bainton**

1 Scottish – nickname; from Scottish Gaelic meaning 'fair(-haired)'.
2 English – nickname; either from Old English meaning 'bone', referring to a tall, skinny person, or from Middle English meaning 'friendly', referring to a sociable person.
3 English – occupational; from Middle English meaning 'bath', referring to someone who worked in a bath house.

Bainbridge

English – place name; from a place in Yorkshire, the name deriving from the River Bain on which it is situated + Old English meaning 'bridge'. Beryl Bainbridge (1934–) is an English novelist.

Baines, Bainton other forms of **Bain**

Baird

Scottish – occupational; possibly from Scottish Gaelic meaning 'poet'. John Logie Baird (1888–1946) was the inventor of television.

Baker

English – occupational; from Old English meaning 'baker'. Dame Janet Baker (1933–) is an English mezzo-soprano.

Bakewell

English – place name; from a place in Derbyshire, the name deriving from an Old English name **Badeca**, itself meaning 'battle' +'spring'.

Bald

Other form: **Bauld**

Scottish – nickname; meaning 'ball' or perhaps 'bold'.

Baldwin

English – personal name; from Germanic meaning 'brave' + 'friend'. Stanley Baldwin (1867–1947) was a British prime minister.

Balfour

Scottish – place name; especially the place in Fife, near Markinch, the name deriving from Old Gaelic meaning 'place of the pasture'. Arthur Balfour (1848–1930) was a British prime minister.

Ball
Other form: **Balle**, **Ballard**
English
1 nickname; from Middle English meaning 'ball', referring either to a short, plump person, or to a bald man whose head resembled a ball,
2 place name; from Middle English meaning 'ball', referring to a round-topped hill.
3 personal name; from an Old Norse name **Balle**, itself from Old Norse meaning 'torture, pain'. J G Ballard (1930–) is a British novelist.

Ballantine
Other form: **Ballantyne**
Scottish – place name; probably from Bellenden in Roxburghshire, which may derive from Scottish Gaelic meaning 'farm of the dean'.

Ballard, **Balle** other forms of **Ball**

Bamford
English – place name; from places in Derbyshire and Lancashire, the name deriving from Old English meaning 'tree, beam, plank' + 'ford', indicating a place where a stream was bridged by a tree trunk.

Bancroft
English – place name; from many small places in England, the name deriving from Old English meaning 'bean' + 'field, smallholding'.

Banister
Other form: **Bannister**
English – occupational; from Old French meaning 'basket maker'. Sir Roger Gilbert Bannister (1929–) is an English neurologist and athlete, the first runner to break the 'four-minute mile'.

Bankes other form of **Banks**

Banks
Other form: **Bankes**
English – place name; from Old Norse meaning 'bank, hillside'.

Bannerman
Scottish – occupational; there is a popular belief that an ancestor was hereditary standard-bearer to the Kings of Scots, but there is no hard evidence for this. The name has been in use since the 14th century.

Bannister other form of **Banister**

Barber
Other form: **Barbour**

English – occupational; from Old French meaning 'barber', a trade
which also included some surgery and dentistry.

Barclay
Other forms: **Berkley**, **Barkley**
English and Scottish – place name; from places in Gloucestershire and
Somerset, the name deriving from Old English meaning 'birch wood'.
John Barclay (1728–1827) founded Barclays Bank.

Barker
English – occupational; from Old Norse meaning 'tanner', from the
occupation of stripping tree bark for the tanning process. Ronnie
Barker (1929–) is an English comic actor.

Barkley other form of **Barclay**

Barlow
English – place name; from places in Lancashire and Yorkshire, the
name deriving from Old English meaning 'barley' + 'hill', though
places in Derbyshire and Shropshire probably derive from Old English
meaning 'barley' + 'wood, clearing'.

Barnard
English – personal name; from a form of the first name **Bernard**, itself
from Germanic meaning 'strength of the bear'.

Barnes
English
1 place name; from (in some cases) Barnes in Surrey, the name
deriving from Middle English meaning 'barn, granary'.
2 occupational; meaning 'young warrior' and used in the Middle Ages
for a member of the upper classes. The name referred to a servant of
such a person.
3 Irish – personal name; anglicized form of Irish Gaelic **Ó Barrane**,
descendant of **Barran**, itself meaning 'spear'.

Barr
Scottish – place name; probably from villages in Ayrshire and
Renfrewshire, the name deriving from Scottish Gaelic meaning 'a hill,
high place'.

Barraclough
Other forms: **Barrowclough**, **Barrowcliff**
English – place name; from a place in Yorkshire, the name deriving
from Old English meaning 'grove' + 'ravine'.

Barratt
Other form: **Barrett**
English
1 personal name; from a Norman-French name probably based on Germanic.
2 nickname; from Middle English meaning 'trouble, deception, cheating', referring to someone dishonest in business.

Barrie other form of **Barry**

Barrowcliff, **Barrowclough** other forms of **Barraclough**

Barry
Other form: **Barrie** (mainly Scottish)
1 English – place name; from Norman-French of Germanic origin meaning 'rampart'.
2 Welsh – personal name; from Welsh 'ap' meaning 'son of' + **Harry**;
3 Scottish – place name; probably from the village of Barry in Angus, the name deriving from Scottish Gaelic meaning 'uppermost part'. J M Barrie (1860–1937) was a Scottish author, best remembered for the play Peter Pan.
4 Irish – personal name; anglicized form of either Irish Gaelic **Ó Beargha**, descendant of **Beargh**, itself meaning 'robber', or else of **Ó Báire**, descendant of **Báire**.

Barson other form of **Bartholomew**

Bartholomew
Other forms: **Barson, Bartlett, Bartle, Barty**
English – personal name; from Hebrew meaning 'son of **Talmai**'.

Barton
English – place name; from many places, the name deriving from Old English meaning 'barley' + 'settlement'.

Barty other form of **Bartholomew**

Barwell
English – place name; from a place in Leicestershire, the name deriving from Old English meaning 'boar' + 'stream'.

Baskerville
English – place name; from a place in Normandy, the name deriving from Old French meaning 'copse' + 'settlement'.

Batchelor other form of **Bachelor**

Bate, **Bateman** other forms of **Bates**

Bates
Other forms: **Bate**, **Bateman**, **Bateson**, **Boatman**, **Bottman**
English
1 personal name; from a familiar form of **Bartholomew**, itself from Hebrew meaning 'son of **Talmai**.'
2 occupational; from Old English meaning 'boat' referring to a boatman.

Baugh
Welsh – nickname; from a diminutive form of Welsh meaning 'dear'.

Bauld other form of **Bald**

Baxendale
English – place name; from Baxenden in Lancashire, the name deriving from Old English meaning 'bake stone, flat stone for bread baking' + 'valley'.

Baxter
English and Scottish – occupational; from Middle English meaning 'baker', referring particularly to a female baker, probably one in charge of a communal bread oven, or a servant employed in a wealthy household.

Beadle
Other forms: **Beddall**, **Biddle**
English – occupational; from Middle English meaning 'court official', referring to the medieval usher in a court of justice whose duties included issuing proclamations.

Beale
English – nickname; from Old French meaning 'beautiful', referring to someone handsome.

Bean
English – occupational/nickname; from Old English meaning 'beans', referring either to a grower or seller of beans, or else referring to someone of little worth, or from Middle English meaning 'friendly', referring to an amiable character.

Beard
English
1 nickname; from Middle English meaning 'beard', referring to someone who wore a beard.
2 place name; from a place in Derbyshire, the name deriving from Old English meaning 'edge' or 'bank'.

Beaton
Scottish – personal name/place name; either from Scottish Gaelic
MacBeatha (also anglicized as **MacBeth**) a Hebridean family of Irish
origin, who were hereditary doctors in the Islands, or from **Bethune**
(still sometimes spelt thus), from the name of the town in NE France.
The two names inevitably became confused.

Beattie
Other form: **Beatty**
Scottish and N Irish – personal name; from **Bate** or **Baty**, a familiar
form of **Bartholomew**, though sometimes thought of as a familiar
form of **Beatrice**.

Bebbington
English – place name; from a place in Cheshire, from Old English
meaning 'settlement associated with **Bebbe**', the latter being a male
and female name of uncertain origin.

Beck
Other forms: **Beckett**, **Beckman**, **Bexon**
English
1 place name; from many places including some in France, the name
deriving from Northern Middle English meaning 'stream'.
2 occupational; from Old English meaning 'pickaxe or mattock',
referring to a maker or user of such tools.

Beddall other form of **Beadle**

Beddis other form of **Beddow**

Beddoes other form of **Beddow**

Beddow
Other forms: **Beddis**, **Beddoes**, **Eddow**, **Eddow(es)**, **Edess**
Welsh – personal name; familiar form of **Bedo**, itself a familiar form
of **Meredydd** meaning 'splendour' + 'lord'.

Begg
Scottish and N Irish – nickname; from Scottish Gaelic meaning
'small'.

Belcher other form of **Bowser**

Bell
Other forms: **Beller**, **Belman**
1 English – occupational/place name; from Old English meaning
'bell', referring to a bellringer or bellfounder, or to a residence near a
bell.

2 English and Scottish – personal name; from the medieval name **Bel**, meaning 'handsome', or from a familiar form of **Isabelle.**

Bellamy
Irish – nickname; from Old French meaning 'fine friend'. David Bellamy (1933–) is a botanist and broadcaster.

Beller, **Belman** other forms of **Bell**

Bellis Welsh form of Ellis

Belman other form of **Bell**

Benbow
English – occupational; from Middle English meaning 'to bend' + 'bow', referring to an archer.

Benedict other form of **Bennett**

Benn
Other forms: **Benny**, **Benson**
English – personal name; from a Middle English name **Benne**, which is a fusion of a short form of **Benedict** and an Old Norse name **Bjorn**, meaning 'bearcub' or 'warrior'. Antony Wedgewood Benn (1925–) is an English Labour politician.

Bennet other form of **Bennett**

Bennett
Other forms: **Bennet**, **Benedict**
English – personal name; from the medieval name **Benedict**, itself from Latin meaning 'blessed'.

Benny, **Benson** other forms of **Benn**

Bentley
English – place name; from numerous places in England, the name deriving from Old English meaning 'bent grass' + ' clearing'.

Berkley other form of **Barclay**

Berriman, **Berry** other forms of **Bury**

Bessant
Other form: **Bezzant**
English – occupational; from Old French based on Latin 'bizantius', a coin deriving its name from Bizantium, the name referring to a maker of coins or a wealthy man.

Bessemer

English – occupational; from Middle English meaning 'broom', referring to a maker of brooms. Sir Henry Bessemer (1813–98) was an English inventor and engineer whose Bessemer converter improved the steel-making process.

Best

English – nickname/occupational; from Middle English meaning 'beast', referring either to someone whose behaviour was violent or savage, or else to someone who looked after animals. George Best (1946–) is an Irish footballer.

Bethell

1 Welsh – personal name; from Welsh 'ap' meaning 'son of' + the name **Ithael** meaning 'bountiful lord'.

2 English – personal name; from a medieval short form of **Beth**, itself a familiar form of **Elizabeth.**

Bethune see **Beaton**.

Bevan

Welsh – personal name; from Welsh 'ap' meaning 'son of' + **Evan**, itself from **Ieuan** a Welsh form of **John.** Aneurin Bevan (1897–1960) was a Labour politician who introduced the National Health Service in 1948.

Bexon other form of **Beck**

Bezzant other form of **Bessant**

Bibby

English – personal name; from **Bibbe**, a short form of **Isabel**, itself a Spanish form of **Elizabeth** from Hebrew meaning 'God is perfection'.

Bickerstaff

Other form: **Bickersteth**

English – place name; from a place near Ormskirk in Lancashire, the name deriving from Old English meaning 'beekeeper' + 'landing place'.

Biddle other form of **Beadle**

Bigg other form of **Biggs**

Biggin

Other form: **Biggins**

English – place name; from various places in England, the name deriving from Middle English meaning 'building' or 'outbuilding'.

Biggs
Other form: **Bigg**
English – nickname; from Old English meaning 'strong, stout'.

Bing
English – personal name; probably from the Old English clan of the Binningas, the people of **Binna.**

Bingley
English – place name; from a place in Yorkshire, the name deriving from either Old English meaning 'hollow' + 'clearing', or else from Old Norse meaning 'refuse heap' + Old English meaning 'clearing'.

Birchall
Other form: **Burchall**
English – place name; from a place in Cheshire, the name deriving from Old English meaning 'nook with birch trees'.

Birt other form of **Burt**

Birtwhistle
English – place name; from a place in Lancashire, the name deriving from Old English meaning 'young bird' + 'stream junction'. Sir Harrison Birtwhistle (1934–) is an English composer and clarinettist.

Bissell
English – occupational; from Middle English meaning 'bushel', referring to someone who measured corn, a corn merchant.

Black
Other forms: **Blackett, Blagg**
English and Scottish – nickname; from Old English meaning 'white' or 'black', referring to a dark or fair person. The Old English words for white and black are so similar that it is hard to determine the origin of names based on them. See also **Blake.**

Blackie
Scottish – nickname; for someone with dark hair or complexion, or for someone reputed to have the power of the evil eye. It was the name of well-known Scottish publishing family.

Blagg other form of **Black**

Blair
Scottish – place name; from several places of this name, from Scottish Gaelic meaning 'plain; battle-field'. Tony Blair (1953–) is a Labour politician and leader of his party.

Blake
Other forms: **Blakeman**, **Bleach**
English – nickname; from Old English meaning 'white' or 'black', referring to a dark, or also fair, person. See **Black.** William Blake (1757–1827) was an English poet and painter.

Blanchflower
English – nickname; from Old French meaning 'white' + 'flower', possibly referring to a man of delicate or effeminate appearance.

Blay other form of **Bliss**

Bleach other form of **Blake**

Bligh
Other forms: **Blight**, **Bly**, **Blythe**
English – nickname; from Old English meaning 'cheerful'. William Bligh (1754–1817) was Captain of the *Bounty* when her mutinous crew set him adrift with a few provisions in an open boat. He survived a 4,000 mile journey ending in East Timor.

Bliss
Other forms: **Blay**, **Ellis**
English
1 nickname; from Old English meaning 'cheerful'.
2 place name; from Blay in France (formerly spelt Bleis).
3 personal name; from Welsh 'ap' meaning 'son of' + **Ellis**.

Blount other form of **Blunt**

Bloxham
English – place name; from places in Oxfordshire and Lincolnshire, the name probably deriving from an Old English name **Blocc** + 'homestead'.

Blundell other form of **Blunt**

Blunt
Other form: **Blount**, **Blundell**
English – nickname; from Norman-French of Germanic origin meaning 'blond', referring to a fair-complexioned or fair-haired person. Anthony Frederick Blunt (1907–83) was a British art historian and Soviet spy.

Bly other form of **Bligh**

Blythe other form of **Bligh**

Boatman other form of **Bates**

Boddington
English – place name; from a place in Northhamptonshire, the name deriving from Old English meaning 'hill of **Bota**.'

Boddy
English
1 nickname; from Middle English meaning 'body', referring to someone of striking appearance.
2 occupational; from Middle English meaning 'messenger'.

Boleyn other form of **Bullen**

Bolger
Other forms: **Bulger, Boulsher**
1 English – occupational; from Middle English meaning 'leather bag', referring to a leather craftsman.
2 Irish – personal name; anglicized form of Irish Gaelic **Ó Bolguidhir**, descendant of **Bolgodhar**, meaning 'belly' + 'yellow'.

Bolt
Other forms: **Boult, Boulter**
English
1 occupational; from Middle English meaning 'to sift', referring to a bolter or sifter of flour.
2 occupational; from Old English meaning 'arrow' or 'bolt', referring to a maker of bolts or bars.

Bone
Other forms: **Boon, Bunn**
English – nickname; either from Old French meaning 'good', referring to someone virtuous or amiable, or from Old English meaning 'bone' referring to a thin person.

Bonham
English
1 nickname/occupational; from Old French meaning 'good man', either referring to qualities of character or to the fact that the person was a peasant farmer or 'bon homme'.
2 place name; possibly from an Old English name **Buna** + 'homestead'.

Boon
Other forms: **Boone, Bown(e)**
English
1 personal name; other form of **Bone**

2 place name; from Bohun in France, of uncertain origin.

Boosey

English – occupational; from Middle English meaning 'cattle stall', referring to a cowherd.

Booth

English – occupational; from Middle English meaning 'small hut', referring to a cowherd or shepherd who lived in such a shelter. William Booth (1829–1912) was an English religious leader and founder of the Salvation Army.

Boothroyd

English – place name; from a place in Yorkshire, the name deriving from Middle English meaning 'hut' + 'clearing'.

Boswell

Scottish – place name; of Norman-French origin, probably deriving from a personal name + 'ville' meaning 'settlement.' James Boswell (1740–95) was the biographer of Dr Samuel Johnson.

Bosworth

English – place name; from a place in Leicestershire, the name deriving from an Old English name **Bosa** + 'enclosure'.

Bothamly other form of **Bottomley**

Botler other form of **Butler**

Bottell other form of **Butler**

Bottle other form of **Butler**

Bottman other form of **Bates**

Bottomley

Other form: **Bothamly**

English – place name; from a place in Yorkshire, the name deriving from Old English meaning 'deep valley' + 'enclosure'.

Bough other form of **Bow**

Boulsher other form of **Bolger**

Boult, Boulter other forms of **Bolt**

Bow

Other forms: **Bowe, Bowes, Bough**

English

1 occupational; from Middle English meaning 'bow', referring to a maker or seller of bows.

2 place name; from Middle English meaning 'bridge'.
3 Irish – personal name; from Irish Gaelic **Ó Buadhaigh**, descendant of **Buadhach**, itself meaning 'victorious'.

Bowen
1 Welsh – personal name; from Welsh 'ap' meaning 'son of' + **Owen**, itself from a Welsh translation of Latin meaning 'well-born'.
2 Irish – personal name; anglicized form of Irish Gaelic **Ó Buadhacháin**, 'descendant of **Buadhach**', itself meaning 'victorious'.

Bowes other form of **Bow**

Bowie
Scottish and Irish – nickname; from Gaelic meaning ' yellow-haired, fair-haired'.

Bown, Bowne other forms of **Boon**

Bowser
Other form: **Belcher**
English – nickname; from Old French meaning 'fine Sir', referring to someone who habitually used the words as a form of address.

Boyce
Other forms: **Boyes, Boyson**
English
1 place name; from Old French meaning 'wood'.
2 nickname; from Germanic meaning 'boy, servant'.

Boyd
Scottish – place name; from the Scottish Gaelic form of Bute, the island in the Firth of Clyde; its origin is obscure.

Boyes other form of **Boyce**

Boyle
1 Irish – personal name; anglicized form of Irish Gaelic **Ó Baoighill**, descendant of **Baio(th)gheall**, probably meaning 'rash' + 'pledge'.
2 Scottish – place name; of Norman-French origin, from Boyville near Caen in Normandy, the name deriving from a personal name + 'settlement'.

Boyson other form of **Boyce**

Bracer other form of **Brasher**

Braddock
English – place name; from Old English meaning 'broad oak'.

Bradlaugh other form of **Bradley**

Bradley
Other forms: **Bradlaugh**, **Bratley**
English and Scottish – place name; from many places, the name deriving from Old English meaning 'broad clearing'.

Bragg
English – nickname; from Middle English meaning 'cheerful, lively'.

Brain
Other forms: **Braine**, **Brayne**
Irish and Scottish – occupational; anglicized form of Irish Gaelic **Mac an Bhreitheamhan**, itself meaning 'son of the judge'. See also **Mac Brayne.**

Bramley
Other form: **Bromley**
English – place name; from many places, the name deriving from Old English meaning 'broom' + 'clearing'.

Brand
Other forms: **Braund**, **Brant**, **Branson**
English – personal name; from the Germanic name **Brando**, meaning 'sword'.

Brandreth
English – place name; from a place in Kent, the name deriving from Old English meaning 'burnt' + 'clearing'.

Branson other form of **Brand**

Brant other form of **Brand**

Brasher
Other form: **Bracer**
English – occupational; either from Old French meaning 'to brew', referring to a brewer, or from Old English meaning 'to cast in brass', referring to a worker in brass.

Bratley other form of **Bradley**

Braund other form of **Brand**

Brayne other form of **Brain**

Brebner other form of **Bremner**

Bremner
Other form: **Brebner**
Scottish – place name/occupational; meaning native of Brabant in the Netherlands. Mainly in the form *brabanar*, it was also used in former

times to mean 'weaver'; many craftsmen from the Low Countries came to Scotland in medieval times.

Brennan
Irish – personal name; anglicized form of Irish Gaelic **Ó Braonáin**, descendant of **Braonán**, itself meaning 'rain drop'.

Bretherton
English – place name; from a place in Lancashire, the name deriving from Old English meaning 'settlement of the brothers'.

Brian
Other forms: **Bryan**, **Brien**, **Bryant**, **O Brien**

English – personal name; originally from Ireland and Brittany as a surname, possibly from Irish Gaelic meaning 'high' or 'noble'.

Brice
Other forms: **Bryce**, **Bryson**

English – personal name; from **Britius**, a Latin form of a Celtic saint's name.

Brindley
English – place name; from a place in Cheshire, the name deriving from Old English meaning 'burnt' + 'clearing'.

Briscoe
Other forms: **Briskey**, **Brisker**

English – place name; from a place in Cumbria, the name deriving from Old Norse meaning 'wood of the Britons'.

Brocklehurst
English – place name; from Middle English meaning 'badger' + 'wooded hill'.

Brodie
Scottish – place name; from the area in Morayshire, itself from Scottish Gaelic, possibly meaning 'heat, boiling'. The Brodie family still live in Brodie Castle near Inverness.

Bromley other form of Bramley

Broughton
English – place name; from numerous places in Britain, the name deriving from Old English meaning 'brook' + 'enclosure'. Alternatively, in some cases, it may be from Old English meaning 'fortress' or 'hill' + 'enclosure'.

Brown

Other forms: **Broun**, **Browne**

English – nickname/personal name; either from Middle English meaning 'brown', or from an Old English name **Brun**, in the first case referring to someone with dark hair or complexion. John Brown (1735–88) was an American anti-slavery campaigner, hanged in Virginia for his activities.

Bruce

Scottish – place name; originally **de Brus**, the name derives from Brix in Normandy. The family came to England with the Norman Conquest and later held lands in Annandale in SW Scotland. King Robert I (1274–1329), known as Robert the Bruce, led the Scots to victory over the English at Bannockburn in 1314. It is the family name of the Earls of Elgin.

Brunton

Scottish and N English – place name; from Old English meaning 'stream' + 'settlement'.

Bryan, **Bryant** other forms of **Brian**

Bryce, **Bryson** other forms of **Brice**

Buchan

Scottish – place name; from the district in Aberdeenshire, itself of doubtful origin. John Buchan was an early 20th-century Scottish novelist and statesman.

Buchanan

Scottish – place name; from the district in Stirlingshire, the name possibly deriving from Scottish Gaelic meaning 'house' + 'canon'. George Buchanan was a 16th-century Latin scholar and poet (and tutor to King James VI). James Buchanan (1791–1868) was 15th president of the USA.

Buckleigh other form of **Buckley**

Buckley

Other form: **Buckleigh**

English – place name; from many areas, the name deriving from Old English meaning 'he-goat' + 'clearing', alternatively, in some cases, from the name **Bow** (meaning 'to bend') + 'cliff', or from Bulkley a Cheshire place name from Old English meaning 'bullock' + 'clearing'.

Buckston, **Buckstone** other forms of **Buxton**

Budgen
Other form: **Budgeon**
English – nickname; from the Norman-French phrase 'Bon Jean', meaning 'good **John**'.

Bulger other form of **Bolger**

Bullant other form of **Bullen**

Bullen
Other forms: **Boleyn, Bullant**
English – place name; from the French port of Boulogne, the name deriving from a Latin name containing the meaning 'good'. Anne Boleyn (1504–36) was the second wife of Henry VlII.

Bulmer
English – place name; from a place in Essex, the name deriving from Old English meaning 'bull' + 'lake'.

Bunn other form of **Bone**

Bunyan
English
1 nickname; from Old French meaning 'swelling', referring to someone with a hump.
2 occupational; from Old French meaning 'high, rounded fruit pie', referring to a confectioner of such pies. John Bunyan (1628–88) was an English writer and preacher, author of *Pilgrim's Progress*.

Burchall other form of **Birchall**

Burgess
English – occupational; from Middle English meaning 'inhabitant, freeman' referring to someone who had certain rights and duties in a town.

Burke
English – place name; from Middle English meaning 'fort', referring particularly to a town based on the site of a hill fort.

Burness other form of **Burns**

Burnet other form of **Burnett**

Burnett
Other form: **Burnet**
Scottish – personal name; originally **Burnard**, itself from an Old English personal name **Beornheard.**

Burnhouse other form of **Burns**

Burns
Other forms: **Burness, Burnhouse**
Scottish and N English – place name; from Middle English meaning 'stream' + 'house'. Robert Burns (1759–96) is the national poet of Scotland.

Burrel other form of **Burrell**

Burrell
Other form: **Burrel**
Scottish – place name; from Burrill in Yorkshire, the name becoming common in the Borders. Sir William Burrell (1861–1958) was a Glasgow shipowner who left his huge art collection to the city.

Burris other form of **Burrows**

Burrough, Burroughs other forms of **Burrows**

Burrow other form of **Burrows**

Burrows
Other forms: **Burris, Burrough(s), Burrow,**
English – place name; from Old English meaning 'hill, tumulus', but also confused with derivatives of Old English meaning 'fort'.

Burt
Other form: **Birt**
English – nickname; from Old English meaning 'bright, shining'.

Burton
English – place name; from Old English meaning 'fort' + 'settlement'.

Bury
Other forms: **Berry, Berriman**
English – place name; from Old English meaning 'fortified place'.

Busby
English – place name; from a place in Yorkshire, the name deriving from Old Norse meaning 'bush' + 'homestead'.

Butler
Other forms: **Botler, Bottell, Bottle**
English and Irish – occupational; from Old French meaning 'bottler', referring to a wine steward, but the post in the Middle Ages had more prestige than the name now suggests, as it was usually held by a high officer in a noble or rich household.

Butterworth

English – place name; from places in Yorkshire and Lancashire, the name deriving from Old English meaning 'butter' + 'enclosure'.

Buxton

Other forms: **Buckston(e)**

English – place name; from the place in Derbyshire, the name deriving from Middle English meaning 'the bowing stones', referring to large boulders which rock when touched.

Byatt

English – place name; from Middle English meaning 'by' + 'gate',

Bygrave

English – place name; from a place in Hertfordshire, the name deriving from Middle English meaning 'by' + 'ditch'.

Byrne

Other form: **O Byrne**

Irish – personal name; anglicized form of Irish Gaelic **Ó Broin**, descendant of **Bran**, itself meaning 'raven'.

Byrom other form of **Byron**

Byron

Other form: **Byrom**

English – occupational; from Old English meaning 'at the cattle sheds', referrring to the job of cowman. George Gordon Byron, 6th Baron Byron of Rochdale (1788–1824), was a Romantic poet, creator of the Byronic hero and a supporter of European revolutionary causes.

C

Cadbury
English – place name; from places in Devon and Somerset, the name deriving from the Old English personal name **Cada** + 'fortress'.

Caddell other form of **Cadell**

Caddick other form of **Caddock**

Caddock
Other forms: **Caddick**, **Cadogan**
1 Welsh – personal name; either from an Old Welsh personal name **Cadoc**, itself meaning 'battle', or from a familiar form of **Caedfel** meaning 'battle' + 'metal'.
2 English – nickname; from Middle English meaning 'fall', referring to a sickly person, or a sufferer from epilepsy, the 'falling sickness'.

Cadell
Other forms: **Caddell**, **Cattell**
Scottish, Welsh and Irish – [in Scotland usually pronounced 'caddle']
1 place name; variant form of **Calder**.
2 personal name; from a Celtic name, itself containing an element meaning 'battle'.

Cadogan other form of **Caddock**

Cadwallader
Welsh – personal name; from an Old Welsh personal name, itself meaning 'battle' + 'leader'. Cadwaladr was a 12th-century Welsh prince of Gwynedd who conquered, then lost, large parts of Wales, eventually regaining his territories with the help of Henry ll of England.

Cahane other form of **Keane**

Cahill
Irish – personal name; anglicized form of Irish Gaelic **Ó Cathail**, descendant of **Cathal**, itself meaning 'battle' + 'strong'.

Cain
English – Other forms: **Cane**, **Caine**, **Caines**, **Kain(e)**, **Kane**, **Kayne** nickname; from Old French meaning 'cane, reed', referring to a thin person. Michael Caine (1933–) is an English film actor.

Caines other form of **Cain** and **Keynes**

Cairnes other form of **Cairns**

Cairns
Other form: **Cairnes**
Scottish – place name; from the lands in Midlothian, the name deriving from Scottish Gaelic meaning 'heap of stones, hill'.

Calcott other form of **Caldicott**

Caldecott other form of **Caldicott**

Calder
Scottish – place name; from various places, for example the villages of East, Mid and West Calder in Midlothian, the name deriving from an old Celtic river name, probably meaning 'hard water'. See also **Cadell**.

Caldicott
Other forms: **Caldecott**, **Calcott**, **Chalcott**, **Colcott**
English – place name; from places in many counties, the name deriving from Old English meaning 'cold' + 'cottage', perhaps indicating an unattended wayside shelter or hut.

Caldwell
Other form: **Coldwell**
English, Scottish and Northern Irish – place name; from various places in England and Scotland, the name deriving from Old English meaning 'cold' + 'spring'.

Callow
1 English – place name; from many places, especially in Derbyshire, the name deriving from Old English meaning 'bald, bare' + 'hill', but in some cases from 'cold' + 'hill'.
2 Manx – personal name; anglicized form of Gaelic **Mac Caolaidhe**, from the first name **Caoladhe**, meaning 'slender'.

Calver
English – place name; from a place in Derbyshire, the name deriving from Old English meaning 'calf ridge', though it has probably been confused with **Calvert** in some cases.

Calvert
English – occupational; from Middle English meaning 'cowherd'.

Cameron

Scottish

1 nickname; The Highland name is probably from Scottish Gaelic meaning 'twisted nose'. The head of Clan Cameron is Cameron of Lochiel (near Fort William), whose ancestors were staunch supporters of the Jacobites in the Risings of the 18th century.

2 place name; The Lowland name is from several places, the name probably deriving from Cambernon in Normandy.

Campbell

Scottish – nickname; from Scottish Gaelic meaning 'twisted mouth'. The Clan Campbell was one of the most powerful in the Highlands and supported the Government against the Jacobites in the 17th and 18th centuries. The head of the clan is the Duke of Argyll.

Cane other form of **Cain**

Cantwell

English – place name; probably from an Old English personal name **Canta** + 'stream'.

Capon

English – occupational/nickname; from Middle English meaning 'castrated cock' referring either to someone who raised poultry, or to a cuckold.

Capp other form of **Capper**

Capper

Other form: **Capp**, **Capps**

English – occupational; from Middle English meaning 'headgear', referring to a maker of caps.

Capstick

English – occupational; from Old French meaning 'cut' + Middle English meaning 'stick', referring to a woodcutter.

Cardew

Other forms: **Carthew**, **Cardy**

English – place name; from places in Cornwall and Cumbria, the name deriving from Old Welsh meaning 'fort' + 'dark'.

Carew

Other form: **Carey**

Welsh – place name; from minor places in Wales, the name deriving from Welsh meaning 'fortress' + 'hill'.

Carey
Other forms: **Keary**, **Keery** (Irish) and **Cary**
1 Welsh – place name; other form of **Carew.**
2 English – place name; either from places in Devon and Somerset, the name deriving from the River Carey, itself from Celtic meaning 'dear', or else from a place in France of unknown origin.
3 Irish – personal name; anglicized form of Irish Gaelic **Ó Ciardha**, descendant of **Ciardha**, itself meaning 'black, dark'.

Carless
Other form: **Corless**
English – nickname; from Old English meaning 'free from grief or care'.

Carlisle
Other form: **Carlyle**
English, Scottish and N Irish – place name; from the town in Cumberland, the name deriving from Old Welsh meaning 'fort' + a Romano-British first name. Thomas Carlyle (1795–1881) was a Scottish writer and historian.

Carman
English
1 personal name; from one form of an Old Norse name **Karlmann**, itself meaning 'man' + 'person'
2 occupational; from Old English meaning 'cart' +'man', referring to a carter.

Carmichael
Scottish – place name; from the parish in Lanarkshire, the name deriving from Old Welsh meaning 'fort' + the first name **Michael**.

Carmode other form of **Kermode**

Carnegie
Scottish – place name; from the lands in Angus, the name deriving from Scottish Gaelic meaning 'fort' + 'gap'. Andrew Carnegie (1835–1908) was a Scottish-American millionaire and philanphropist.

Carr
1 English and Scottish – Other form of **Kerr**
2 Irish – personal name; anglicized form of either Irish Gaelic **Ó Carra**, descendant of **Carra**, meaning 'spear', or else of Irish Gaelic **Mac Giolla Chathair**, son of the servant of **Cathar**, itself meaning 'battle'.

Carrol other form **Carroll**

Carroll
Other form: **Carrol**
Irish – personal name; anglicized form of Irish Gaelic **Cearbhall**, possibly meaning 'to hack, to butcher'.

Carruthers
Scottish – place name; from the lands in Dumfries-shire, the name deriving from Old Welsh meaning 'fort' + a personal name.

Carson
Scottish and N Irish – place name; of obscure origin, it was the name of a prominent family in Galloway in the Middle Ages. Rachel Louise Carson (1907–64) was an American naturalist and science writer famous for her revelations about environmental pollution in *Silent Spring* (1962).

Carswell
Scottish – place name; from the place in Renfrewshire, the name deriving from Scots meaning 'river meadow' + 'well',

Carthew other form of **Cardew**

Cartwright
English – occupational; from Middle English 'cart' + 'wright' meaning 'a maker of carts'.

Carver
English – occupational; either from Middle English meaning 'to carve', referring to a sculptor, or from Norman-French of Germanic origin meaning 'cart, plough', referring to a ploughman.

Cary other form of **Carey**

Casey
Other form: **O Casey**
Irish – personal name; anglicized form of Irish Gaelic **Ó Cathasaigh**, descendant of **Cathusach**, itself meaning 'vigilant' or 'noisy'. Sean O'Casey (1894–1964) was an Irish playwright.

Cash other form of **Cass**

Cass
Other form: **Cash**
English – personal name; from a short form of the medieval name **Cassandra**, itself of uncertain origin. Johnny Cash (1932–) is an American singer.

Catchpole
English – occupational; from Norman-French of Germanic origin meaning 'seize poultry', referring to a bailiff with powers to seize livestock from anyone who did not pay his taxes.

Cater
Other forms: **Chater**, **Chaytor**
English – occupational; from Norman-French of Germanic origin meaning 'receiver, buyer', referring to someone in charge of provisions for a great household.

Cattell other form of **Cadell**

Cavanagh, **Cavanaugh** other forms of **Kavanagh**

Cavendish
English – place name; from a place in Suffolk, the name deriving from an Old English name **Cafna**, itself meaning 'bold' + 'enclosure'.

Cawood
[often pronounced **kay-**wood]
English – place name; from places in Yorkshire and Lancashire, the name deriving from Old English meaning 'jackdaw' + 'wood'.

Cawthorne
English – place name; from places in Yorkshire, the name deriving from Old English meaning 'cold' + 'thorn'.

Cecil
English – personal name; from the first name, itself from Latin meaning 'blind'.

Chaddock other form of **Chadwick**

Chadwick
Other forms: **Chaddock**, **Shaddock**
English – place name; from various places, the name deriving, in the case of places in Worcestershire and Warwickshire, from Old English meaning 'dairy farm' + the name **Ceadel**. However, another place in Worcestershire and one in Lancashire are from Old English meaning 'dairy farm of **Ceadda (Chad)**'. Roy Chadwick (1893–1947) was an English aeronautical engineer who designed many famous wartime aeroplanes.

Chalcot other form of **Caldicott**

Chalice other form of **Challis**

Challen other form of **Challon**

Challes other form of **Challis**

Challis
Other forms: **Challes, Chal(l)ice**
English – place name; from a place in France in Pas de Calais, the name deriving from Old French meaning 'ladders'.

Challon
Other form: **Challen**
English – place name; from places in France, the name deriving from a Gaulish tribal name.

Chalmers Scottish form of **Chambers.**

Chamberlain
Other form: **Chamberlin**
English – occupational; from Norman-French of Germanic origin meaning 'chamber, room', referring originally to a servant who was in charge of his master's private rooms, but the status of the post increased until it denoted a high-ranking official. See also **Chambers.** Arthur Neville Chamberlain (1869–1940) was an English statesman, infamous for his policy of appeasing Adolf Hitler during his time as British prime minister (1937–40).

Chambers
Other form: **Chalmers** (Scottish)
occupational; referring to someone in charge of his master's private rooms (as with **Chamberlain**, but this term never referred to a high-ranking official).

Champney
English – nickname; from Champagne in France, referring to someone from that region.

Chandler
Other form: **Chantler**
English – occupational; from Middle English meaning 'candler', referring to a candlemaker, a seller of candles, or a servant who saw to the lighting in a large household. Raymond Chandler (1988–59) was an American writer of detective stories.

Chapman
English – occupational; from Middle English meaning 'trader, seller'.

Charlesworth
English – place name; from a place in Derbyshire, the name deriving

from an Old English name meaning 'jaw' + 'enclosure', but because of a similarity of sound, the first part has been mistakenly understood as **Charles.**

Charlton
English – place name; from numerous places, the name deriving from Old English meaning 'free peasant, villein' + 'settlement'. Bobby Charlton (1937–) is an English footballer.

Charteris
English – place name; from Chartres in France, the name deriving from an Old French name of a Gaulish tribe.

Chater other form of **Cater**

Chatterley
English – place name; from a place in Staffordshire, the name probably deriving from Celtic meaning 'high hill' + Old English meaning 'wood, clearing'.

Chatwin other form of **Chetwynd**

Chaucer
English – occupational; from Old French meaning 'leggings' or 'footwear', referring to a maker or seller of leggings and slippers. Geoffrey Chaucer was a 14th-century writer, the first great English poet, famous in particular for the *Canterbury Tales*.

Chaytor other form of **Cater**

Checkley
English – place name; from places in Herefordshire, Staffordshire and Cheshire, the name deriving from Old English names, **Ceacca** or **Ceaddica** + 'clearing'.

Cheever
Other forms: **Cheverill, Chivers**
English – nickname; from Norman-French of Germanic origin meaning 'goat', referring to a capricious, obstinate person.

Chegwin
English – place name; from Cornish meaning 'white' + 'house'.

Chetwynd
Other form: **Chatwin**
English – place name; from a place in Shropshire, the name deriving from the Old English name **Ceatta** + 'winding slope'.

Cheverill other form of **Cheever**

Chew
Other form: **Chue**
English
1 place name; from places in Somerset and Yorkshire, the former possibly from Old Welsh meaning 'young bird', the latter from Old English meaning 'ravine'.
2 nickname; from Old English meaning 'chough', a bird like a jackdaw, referring to a noisy, thieving person.

Chippendale
English – place name; from Old English meaning 'trading' + 'valley'. Thomas Chippendale (1718–89) was an English furniture designer and maker.

Chisholm
Scottish – place name; from the lands in Roxburghshire, the name possibly deriving from Old English meaning 'cheese' + 'meadow'. By the 14th century some of the family had moved to the north and that group became a Highland clan, based near Inverness.

Chitty
English
1 nickname; from Middle English meaning 'puppy, cub'.
2 place name; from places in Kent and Hampshire, the name deriving from an Old Welsh hill name + Old English meaning 'clearing'.

Chivers other form of **Cheever**

Cholmondley [pronounced **chum-**ley]
Other form: **Chumley**
English – place name; from a place in Cheshire, the name deriving from an Old English name **Ceolmund**, meaning 'ship' + 'protection' + 'clearing'.

Christian
English – personal name; from the first name, itself from Latin meaning 'Christian'.

Christie
Other form: **Christy**
Scottish – personal name; from a familiar form of **Christopher** or **Christian.**

Christopher
English – personal name; from the first name, itself from Greek meaning 'the bearer of Christ'.

Christy other form of **Christie**

Chubb
English – nickname; from Middle English meaning 'chub', a short, broad slow-moving fish, referring to the character or appearance of a person. The word 'chubby' has a similar origin.

Chue other form of **Chew**

Chumley other form of **Cholmondley**

Churchill
English – place name; from Devonshire, Oxfordshire, Somersetshire and Worcestershire, the name deriving from Old English meaning 'church' + 'hill'. The statesman Sir Winston Spencer Churchill (1875–1965), British prime minister during the second World War, was the most famous bearer of the name.

Churton
English – place name; from a place in Cheshire, the name deriving from Old English meaning 'church' + 'settlement'.

Clancy
Other form: **Glancy**
Irish – personal name; anglicized form of Irish Gaelic **Mac Flannchaid**, from the personal name **Flannchadh**, itself meaning 'red' + 'warrior'.

Clapham
English – place name; from places in London, Sussex and Bedfordshire, the name deriving from Old English meaning 'hillock' + 'homestead'.

Clapton
English – place name; from many places including one in London, the name deriving from Old English meaning 'hillock' + 'settlement'.

Clarage other form of **Claridge**

Clarges
English – occupational; from Middle English meaning 'clergyman', referring to the servant of a clergyman.

Claridge
Other form: **Clarage**
English
1 personal name; from the Middle English name **Clarice**, itself from Latin meaning 'bringer of fame'.
2 place name; from Clearhedge, a place in Sussex of uncertain origin.

Clark

Other forms: **Clarke**, **Clarkson**

English – occupational; from Old English meaning 'priest', referring to a member of a minor religious order, a scribe, or a secretary.

Claypole

English – place name; from a place in Lincolnshire, the name deriving from Old English meaning 'clay' + 'pool'.

Clayton

English – place name; from places in Lancashire, Yorkshire and Derbyshire, the name deriving from Old English meaning 'clay' (used for pottery) + 'settlement'.

Cleary

Irish – occupational; from Irish Gaelic meaning 'clerk'.

Cleaver

Other form: **Clover**

English – occupational; from Old English meaning 'to split, to cut', referring to someone who cut wood into planks.

Cleeve, **Cleeves** other forms of **Clive**

Clegg

English – place name; from a place in Lancashire, the name deriving from Old Norse meaning 'haystack'.

Cleland

Other form: **Clelland**

Scottish – place name; from the area in Lanarkshire, the name probably deriving from Old English meaning 'clay' + 'land'.

Clement

Other forms: **Clements**, **Clementson**, **Clemson** (Cornish)

English – personal name; from the first name, itself from Latin meaning 'merciful'.

Clemson Cornish form of **Clement**

Clewe, **Clewes** other forms of **Clough**

Cliff, **Cliffe** other form of **Clive**

Clifford

English – place name; from places in Gloucestershire, Herefordshire and Yorkshire, the name deriving from Old English meaning 'cliff' + 'ford'. The name only became a first name in the 20th century.

Clinton

English – place name; from Glympton in Oxfordshire, the name deriving from Old English meaning 'settlement on the River Glyne'. A famous bearer of the name is William Clinton, president of the United States in the 1990s.

Clive

Other forms: **Cliff(e)**, **Cleeve(s)**

English – place name; from places in Shropshire and Cheshire, the name deriving from Old English meaning 'slope, bank'.

Close

English – place name/nickname; either from Old English meaning 'enclosure', or else from Old Norse meaning 'reserved, cautious'.

Clough

Other forms: **Clowe(s)**, **Clewe(s)**

English – place name; from Old English meaning 'ravine'. Arthur Hugh Clough (1819–61) was an English poet.

Clover other form of **Cleaver**

Clowe, Clowes other forms of **Clough**

Clyde

Scottish – place name; from the river name, itself of ancient origin, probably the name of a river goddess meaning 'one who cleans, washes'.

Coates

1 English – Other form: **Coats, Cotman**

place name; from many places, for example, Cambridgeshire and Leicestershire, the name deriving from Middle English meaning 'cottage'.

2 Scottish – place name; other form of **Coutts.**

Cobden

English – place name; from a place in Yorkshire, the name probably deriving from Old English meaning 'lump' + 'hill'. Richard Cobden (1804–65) was an English economist and politician who advocated free trade.

Cochran other form of **Cochrane**

Cochrane

Other form: **Cochran**

Scottish – place name; from the lands in Renfrewshire, the name of obscure origin, the first element possibly from Old Welsh meaning 'red'.

Cock other form of **Cox**

Cockburn
Scottish – [pronounced '**co**-burn']
place name; from the lands in Berwickshire, the name possibly deriving from Old English meaning 'cuckoo' + 'stream'. Lord Cockburn (1799–1854) was a Scottish judge, politician and writer.

Cocks other form of **Cox**

Coe
English – nickname; from Southern Old English meaning 'jackdaw', referring to someone odd or unusual, or in some way resembling the bird. Sebastian Coe is a well-known 20th-century runner.

Coffey
Irish – personal name; anglicized form of Irish Gaelic **Ó Cobhthaigh**, descendant of **Cobhthach**, itself meaning 'victorious'.

Colcott other form of **Caldicott**

Coldwell see **Caldwell.**

Coleman
Irish
1 personal name; from the Irish personal name **Colmán**, itself from Latin meaning 'dove'.
2 personal name; anglicized form of Irish Gaelic **Ó Clúmháin**, descendant of **Clúmh**, itself meaning 'hair, down'.
3 English – occupational; from Middle English meaning 'charcoal burner, coal man'.

Coleridge
English – place name; from places in Devon, the name deriving from Old English meaning 'charcoal' + 'ridge'. Samuel Taylor Coleridge (1772–1834) was a famous 19th-century poet.

Colin other form of **Collins**

Collins
Other forms: **Colin, Collis, Colli(n)son**
1 English – personal name; from **Coll**, itself a familiar form of **Nicholas** from Greek meaning 'victory' + 'people'.
2 personal name; anglicized form of Irish Gaelic **Ó Coileain**, descendant of **Coileán**, itself meaning 'puppy'.

Colquhoun

Scottish – [pronounced 'ca-**hoon**']
place name; from the lands in Dunbartonshire, the name deriving from
Scottish Gaelic, possibly meaning 'corner' + 'narrow'. (The -quh- is a
survival of an Older Scots spelling now represented as '-wh-'). The
Colquhouns of Luss have held lands on Loch Lomondside since the
13th century.

Coltart other form of **Coulthard**

Colthard other form of **Coulthard**

Condliffe other form of **Cunliffe**

Congreve

English – place name; from a place in Staffordshire, the name deriving
from Old English meaning 'short valley' + 'thicket'. William
Congreve (1670–1729) was an English dramatist and poet.

Conley other form of **Connolly**

Connally other form of **Connolly**

Connell

Other forms: **O Connell**, **Gunnell**
Irish – personal name; anglicized form of Irish Gaelic **Ó Conaill**,
descendant of **Conall**, possibly meaning 'hound' + 'valour'. Daniel
O'Connell (1775–1847) was an Irish political leader known as the
'liberator'.

Connelly other form of **Connolly**

Connolly

Other forms: **Connelly**, **Connally**, **Conley**
Irish – personal name; anglicized form of Irish Gaelic **Ó
Conghalaigh**, descendant of **Conghalach**, itself meaning 'brave',

Connor

Other forms: **Connors**, **O Connor**
Irish – personal name; anglicized form of Irish Gaelic **Ó
Conchobhair**, descendant of **Conchobhar**, itself meaning 'hound' +
'desire'.

Conyers

English – place name; from places in France, the name deriving from
Old French meaning 'quince trees'.

Cooper
Other forms: **Coupe**, **Coupar**
English – occupational; from Middle English meaning 'tub', referring to the job of making vats, casks and other containers.

Cope
English – occupational; from Middle English meaning 'cape', referring to a maker of cloaks and capes.

Coplestone
English – place name; from a place in Devon, the name deriving from Old English possibly meaning 'peaked or pointed stone'.

Corbett
English – nickname; from Norman-French of Germanic origin meaning 'little crow'.

Corcoran
Irish – personal name; anglicized form of Irish Gaelic **Ó Corcráin**, descendant of **Corcrán**, itself meaning 'purple'.

Corless other form of **Carless**

Cosgrave other form of **Cosgrove**

Cosgrove
Other form: **Cosgrave**
1 English – place name; from a place in Northamptonshire, the name deriving from Old English meaning 'grove, thicket'.
2 Irish – personal name; anglicized form of Irish Gaelic **Ó Cosgraigh**, descendant of **Coscrach**, itself meaning 'victorious'.

Cotman other form of **Coates**

Cotter
Other form: **Cotterell**
English – occupational; from Old French meaning 'villein, cottager holding a cottage in return for labour'.

Cottle
Other forms: **Cuttle(s)**, **Cutler**
English
1 occupational; from Old French meaning 'knife', referring to a cutler or possibly a maker of chain mail.
2 place name; from Cotehele in Cornwall, the name deriving from Cornish meaning 'wood by the estuary'.

Coulthard
Other forms: **Colthard**, **Coltart**
English – occupational; from Old English meaning 'colt, ass' + 'herd', referring to someone who looked after work horses and asses.

Coupar other form of **Cooper**

Coupe other form of **Cooper**

Court
Other forms: **A'Court**, **Curt**, **Curzon**
English – occupational/place name; from Middle English meaning 'court, yard', referrring either to a place where there was such an enclosure, or to a person employed in the courtyard of a great house. See also **Curzon.**

Courtenay
Other form: **Court(e)ney**
English
1 nickname; from Old French meaning 'short nose', referring to someone with a snub nose.
2 place name; from a place in Loiret, France, the name deriving from a Roman name **Curtenus**, from Latin meaning 'short'.
3 Irish – personal name; anglicized form of Irish Gaelic **Ó Curnáin**, descendant of **Curnáin**, itself possibly meaning 'ringletted' (of hair).

Cousin other form of **Cousins**

Cousins
Other forms: **Cousin**, **Cusson(s)**, **Cushing**
English – nickname; from Middle English meaning 'cousin, relative', referring to a relative of an important person, or to someone who often used the term as a form of address.

Coutts
Other form: **Coates**
Scottish – place name; from Cults near Aberdeen, the name possibly from Scottish Gaelic meaning 'corner'. The London banking family is descended from a Montrose branch of the family.

Cowan
Other form: **Cowen**
Scottish – personal name/occupational; probably derived from one or more Scottish Gaelic names, though some believe it to be from a Scots word meaning 'builder of drystone walls'.

Coward

English – occupational; from Middle English meaning 'cowherd'. Sir Noel Pierce Coward (1899–1973) was an English actor, dramatist and composer of light music.

Cowdray

English – place name; from places in France and in Sussex, the name deriving from Old French meaning 'hazel copse'.

Cowen other form of **Cowan**.

Cox

Other forms: **Coxe, Cock(s), Coxon**

English

1 nickname; either from Old Welsh meaning 'red', or else from Old English meaning 'cockerel', often referring to a 'cocky' young man, which in turn was the origin of the use of 'cock' as a diminutive, to form names such as **Hancock**.

2 occupational; from Old French meaning 'ship's boat', referring to a sailor.

3 place name; from Old English meaning 'hillock' or 'heap'.

Crabbe

Other form: **Crabtree**

English

1 place name; from Middle English meaning 'crab-apple tree'.

2 nickname; from Middle English meaning 'crab', referring to someone who walked like a crab.

Craddock

Welsh – personal name; from **Caradog**, itself based on an Old Welsh name meaning 'amiable'.

Craig

Scottish – place name; from many places in Scotland of this name, deriving from Scottish Gaelic meaning 'rock'.

Crane

English – nickname; from Old English meaning 'crane', referring to a long-legged thin person like the bird.

Cranfield

English – place name; from many places, the name deriving from Old English meaning 'crane' + 'open land'.

Crankshaw

English – place name; from a place in Lancashire, the name deriving from Old English meaning 'crane' + 'wood'.

Craufurd other form of **Crawford**

Craven

English – place name; from a place in Yokshire, the name deriving from Old Welsh meaning 'garlic'.

Crawford

Other forms: **Craufurd**, **Crawfurd**

Scottish and English – place name; from Old English meaning 'crow' + 'ford', in many cases originating from the lands in Lanarkshire.

Crawley other form of **Crowley**

Creighton other form of **Crichton**

Crewes other form of **Cruise**

Crichton

Other forms: **Creighton**, **Crighton**

Scottish – place name; from the lands in Midlothian, the name deriving from Scottish Gaelic meaning 'boundary' + Scots/Old English meaning 'settlement'. James Crichton, known as 'the Admirable Crichton', was a 16th-century Scottish scholar and poet, whose spectacular exploits ended in a fight with the son of the Duke of Mantua.

Cripps other form of **Crisp**

Crisp

Other form: **Cripps**

English – nickname; from Middle English meaning 'curl', referrring to someone with curly hair. Sir Stafford Cripps (1889–1952) was a Labour statesman and economist.

Critchley

Other form: **Crutchley**

English – place name; from Old English meaning 'cross' + 'clearing'.

Cromwell

English – place name; from places in Nottinghamshire and Yorkshire, the name deriving from Old English meaning 'crooked' + 'stream'. Oliver Cromwell (1599–1658) was an English soldier and statesman who became lord protector of England in 1653.

Crookshanks see **Cruikshank**.

Crosby
Other form: **Crosbie**

English – place name; from several places in S Scotland and N England, the name deriving from Old English meaning 'cross' + 'settlement'. Bing Crosby was the stage name of Harry Lillis (1904–77), American crooner and film star.

Cross
English – place name; from Old English and Old Norse meaning 'cross', referring to a roadside cross or crossroads.

Crowder other form of **Crowther**

Crowley
Other form: **Crawley**

English – place name; from many places in England, the name deriving from Old English meaning 'crow' + 'clearing'.

Crowther
Other form: **Crowder**

English – occupational; from Middle English meaning 'a player on the crowd' (a musical instrument popular in the Middle Ages).

Cruickshank
Other forms: **Cruikshanks**, **Crookshanks**

Scottish – nickname/place name; The obvious explanation, that this was a nickname for someone with crooked legs, has been challenged by the theory that it is derived from a place name (though there is no evidence of this in Scotland).

Cruise
Other forms: **Crews**, **Cruse**

English

1 nickname; from Middle English meaning 'bold, fierce'.

2 place name; from a place in France, the name deriving from Gaulish meaning 'hard'.

Crutchley other form of **Critchley**

Cullen
1 Scottish – place name; from the town in Banffshire, the name probably deriving from Scottish Gaelic meaning 'little corner'.

2 Irish – personal name; anglicized form of either **Ó Cuilinn**, descendant of **Cuileann**, itself meaning 'holly', or else of **Ó Coileáin**, descendant of **Coileán**, itself meaning 'puppy'.

3 English – place name; from the German city of Cologne.

Culpeper other form of **Culpepper**

Culpepper
Other form: **Culpeper**
English – occupational; from Middle English meaning 'to pick' +
'pepper', referring to a herbalist. Nicholas Culpeper (1616–54) was an
English physician and author of an influential work on herbalism.

Cumming other form of **Cummings**

Cummings
Other forms: **Cumming**, **Cummins**
English, Irish and Scottish – personal name; from a Breton name, itself
meaning 'crooked, bent'. The theory that the name comes from
Comines in Normandy is difficult to substantiate.

Cunliffe
Other forms: **Condliffe**, **Cunnliffe**
English – place name; from a place in Lancashire near Rishton, the
name deriving from Old English meaning 'split' + 'cliff'.

Cunningham
Other form: **Cunninghame**
1 Scottish – place name; from the district in Ayrshire, the name of
uncertain origin.
2 Irish – personal name; anglicized form of Irish Gaelic **Ó
Cunneagáin**, descendant of **Cuinneagán**, itself from **Conn** meaning,
'leader, chief'.

Currie
1 Scottish – place name; probably from Corrie in Dumfries-shire, the
name deriving from Scottish Gaelic meaning 'cauldron, hollow on
hillside'. There is no evidence for the name being connected with
Currie in Midlothian.
2 Irish – personal name; anglicized form of Irish Gaelic **Ó
Comhraidhe**, descendant of **Comhraidhe**, of uncertain origin, or of
Ó Corra, descendant of **Corra**, meaning 'spear'.

Curt other form of **Court**

Curtis
English – nickname; either from Middle English meaning 'refined',
referring to a polite person, or from Middle English meaning 'short' +
'hose', referring to a short-legged person or one who wore short
leggings.

Curzon

English

1 occupational; from a diminutive of the surname **Court**, itself from Middle English meaning 'yard, enclosure', referring to someone employed by the lord of a manor.

2 place name; from a place in Normandy, the name deriving from the Roman name **Curtius**, itself from Latin meaning 'short'.

Cushing other form of **Cousin**

Cusson, **Cussons** other forms of **Cousins**

Cuthbert

Other form: **Cuthbertson**

English – personal name; from the first name, itself from Old English meaning 'famous' + 'bright'.

Cutler

English – occupational; from Middle English meaning 'knife', referring to a maker of knives. See also **Cottle**.

D

Dacre
English – place name; from a place in Cumbria, the name deriving from an Old Welsh river name meaning 'trickling'.

Dadd other form of **Dodd**

Dade Irish form of **David**

Daffey Welsh form of **David**

Dafydd Welsh form of **David**

Daile other form of **Dale**

Daintith
Other forms: **Dainty**, **Dentith**
English – nickname; from Middle English meaning 'pleasure' or 'tasty morsel', referring to a well-liked person.

Dakin other form of **Day**

Dalby
English – place name; from places in Yorkshire, Leicestershire and Lincolnshire, the name deriving from Old Norse meaning 'valley' + 'settlement.'

Dale
Other forms: **Daile**, **Deal**
English – place name; from numerous small places, the name deriving from Old Norse meaning 'valley'.

Dalgleish
Other forms: **Dalgliesh**, **Dalglish**
Scottish – place name; from the lands in Selkirkshire, the name deriving from Scottish Gaelic meaning 'field' + 'greyish-green'.

Dalrymple
Scottish – place name; from the place in Ayrshire, the name possibly deriving from Scottish Gaelic meaning 'meadow of the crooked stream'. It is the family name of the Earls of Stair, whose ancestor, later the first earl, played a prominent part in the massacre of Glencoe in 1692.

Dalton
Other forms: **Daughton, Daulton. Dawton**
English – place name; either from many places in England, the name deriving from Old English meaning 'valley' + 'settlement', or else from French meaning 'of, from' + Autun, a place in France.

Dalyell other form of **Dalziel**

Dalziel
Other form: **Dalyell**
Scottish – [pronounced 'dee-**ell**']
place name; from the lands in Lanarkshire, the name deriving from Scottish Gaelic meaning 'at the white field'. In the 17th century General Tam Dalyell of the Binns (in West Lothian) was a scourge of the Covenanters; his descendant and namesake is a Labour politician.

Damper other form of **Dampier**

Dampier
Other form: **Damper**
English – place name; from a place in France, the name deriving from an Old French title of respect 'Dam' or 'Don' + **Pierre**, the place being named after St Peter.

Dando
Other form: **Dannow**
English – place name; from a place in Normandy, the name deriving from Old French meaning 'of, from' + 'alder grove'.

Dandy other form of **Andrew**

Dangerfield
English – place name; from various places in France, the name deriving from French meaning 'of, from ' + Angerville, itself from an Old Norse name meaning 'god' + 'spear' + 'settlement'.

Daniel
Other forms: **Daniels, Daniell**
English – personal name; from the first name, itself from Hebrew meaning 'God has judged'.

Dannow other form of **Dando**

Darcey other form of **Darcy**

Darcy
Other form: **Darcey**
1 English – place name; from a place in la Manche, France, the name

deriving from a Gaulish name, possibly meaning 'bear'.
2 Irish – personal name; anglicized form of Irish Gaelic **Ó Dorchaidhe**, 'descendant of the dark man'.

Darell

Other form: **Dorrell**

English – place name; from a place in Normandy, the name deriving from Latin meaning 'courtyard'.

Darley

English – place name; from two places in Derbyshire, the name deriving from Old English meaning 'deer' + 'clearing'.

Darwin

English

1 personal name; from **Deorwine**, itself from Old English meaning 'dear' + 'friend'.

2 place name; from a place in Lancashire, the name deriving from the river on which it stands, the Derwent. Charles Robert Darwin (1809–82) was an English naturalist, originator of the theory of evolution by natural selection.

Dashwood

English – place name; from Norman-French meaning 'of, from' + Middle English meaning 'ashwood'.

Daughton other form of **Dalton**

Daulton other form of **Dalton**

David

Other forms: **Dade** (Irish), **Daffey**, **Dafydd**, **Dewi** (Welsh), **Davie**, **Davies**, **Davis**, **Davidson**, **Davison**, **Davy**

English – personal name; from the first name, itself from Hebrew meaning 'beloved'.

Daw

Other forms: **Dawe**, **Dawes**, **Dawkins**, **Dawson**

English – personal name; from a familiar form of **David**. See **David**.

Dawton other form of **Dalton**

Day

Other forms: **Dakin**, **Dey**, **Dayman**, **Deason**

English

1 personal name; from a familiar form of **David**.

2 personal name; from a Middle English name **Daye** or **Deye**, itself probably meaning 'day'.

De Lacey other form of **Lacey**

Deacon other form of **Deakin**

Deadman other form of **Debenham**

Deakin
Other form: **Deacon**
English – occupational; from Middle English of Greek origin meaning 'servant', referring to a deacon in the church who was supposed to remain celibate. The name may refer to the servant of a deacon rather than a son.

Deal other form of **Dale**

Deason other form of **Day**

Debenham
Other form: **Debnam**, **De(a)dman**
English – place name; from a place in Suffolk, the name deriving from Old English meaning 'deep' + 'homestead'.

Deemer other form of **Dempster**

Deighton
English – place name; from places in Yorkshire, the name deriving from Old English meaning 'ditch' + 'enclosure'.

Delafield other form of **Field**

Delaney
Irish – personal name; anglicized form of Irish Gaelic **Ó Dubhshláine**, descendant of **Dubhshláine**, itself meaning 'black' + 'challenge, defiance'.

Dempsey
Irish – personal name; anglicized form of Irish Gaelic **Ó Díomasaigh**, descendant of **Díomasach**, itself meaning 'proud, arrogant'.

Dempster
Other forms: **Deemer**, **Dome**
Scottish, Manx and English – occupational; from Old English meaning 'judge', referring to a judge who arbitrated in minor disputes.

Dench
Other forms: **Dennish**, **Denns**, **Dennis**, **Dennys**
English – nickname; from Middle English meaning 'Danish'.

Denes other form of **Dennis**

Denis other form of **Dennis**

Dennett other form of **Dennis**

Dennis

Other forms: **Denis, Denes, Dinnis, Denny, Dennett, Tenney**

English

1 personal name; from the first name, itself from **Dionysius**, the Latin form of the name of the Greek god of wine.

2 personal name; other form of **Dench.**

3 Irish – personal name; anglicized form of **Donohue.**

Dennish, Denns, Dennys other forms of **Dench**

Denny other form of **Dennis**

Dentith other form of **Daintith**

Dermott see **Kermode**

Devereux

English – place name; from Norman-French meaning 'of, from' + Evreux in Normandy.

Dewar

Scottish

1 occupational; from Scottish Gaelic meaning 'pilgrim'; families of this name were hereditary keepers of the relics of a saint. The name is common in Perthshire where it is known from the makers of a famous brand of whisky.

2 place name; from two places in Midlothian (possibly of the same origin as **1**).

Dewhurst

English – place name; from a place in Lancashire, the name deriving from Middle English meaning 'dewy' + 'wooded hill'.

Dewi Welsh form of **David**

Dey other form of **Day**

Diamand, Diamant other forms of **Diamond**

Diamond

Other forms: **Diamand, Diamant**

English – personal name; from a mistaken form of **Dayman.** See **Day.**

Dick

Other forms: **Dickins, Dickens, Diggen, Diggan, Dickson, Dix, Dixon, Dickinson**

English – personal name; from a familiar form of **Richard**, itself from Germanic meaning 'strong ruler'.

Digby
English – place name; from a place in Lincolnshire, the name deriving from Old English meaning 'dyke' + Old Norse meaning 'farm'.

Diggan, **Diggen** other forms of **Dick**

Dilks other form of **Dillon**

Dillon
Other form: **Dilks**
English
1 personal name; from the Germanic name **Dillo**, itself possibly from Germanic meaning 'to destroy'.
2 place name; from a place in Herefordshire, the name deriving from Old English meaning 'retreat'.
2 Irish – personal name; anglicized form of Irish Gaelic **Ó Duilleáin**, descendant of **Duilleán**, possibly meaning 'blind man'.

Dimbleby
English – place name; from a place in Lincolnshire, the name probably deriving from Old Norse meaning 'ravine with water in it' + 'settlement'. Richard Dimbleby (1913–65) was an English broadcaster,as are his sons, well-known for his reporting of state occasions.

Dinnis other form of **Dennis**

Disney
English – place name; from French meaning 'of, from' + Isigny, a place in Calvados, France, the name deriving from a Latin personal name **Isinius**. Walt Disney (1901–66) was an American artist and film maker, creator of Mickey Mouse and many cartoon characters.

Dix other form of **Dick**

Dixey other form of **Dixie**

Dixie
Other form: **Dixey**
English
1 personal name; from **Dick**, itself a familiar form of **Richard.**
2 occupational; from Latin 'dixi' (I spoke), the opening word of the 39th Psalm, referring to the occupation of chorister.

Dixon other form of **Dick**

Dobb other form of **Dobbs**

Dobbs
Other forms: **Dobb, Dobson**
English – personal name; from the medieval name **Dobbe**, itself a
familiar form of **Robert**, from Old English meaning 'fame' + 'bright'.

Docherty
Other form: **Doherty**
Irish and Scottish – personal name; anglicized form of Irish Gaelic **Ó
Dochartaigh**, descendant of **Dochartach**, itself meaning 'unlucky'.

Dod other form of **Dodd**

Dodd
Other forms: **Dodds, Dodson, Dodman, Dadd**
English – personal name; from a medieval name **Dodde**, possibly
from Germanic meaning 'round' or 'plump'.

Dodgson
English – personal name; from a medieval name **Dogge**, itself a
familiar form of **Roger.**

Dodman other form of **Dodd**

Dodson other form of **Dodd**

Doherty other form of **Docherty**

Dome other form of **Dempster**

Donachie Scottish form of **Donohue**

Donald
Other forms: **Donaldson, Donnell, O Donnell**
Scottish and Irish – personal name; from Scottish Gaelic meaning
'world power'. See also **MacDonald.**

Donat
Other forms: **Doney, Don(n)ett**
English – personal name; from a medieval name **Donat** from Latin
meaning 'given',

Donnell other form of **Donald**

Donnelly
Irish – personal name; anglicized form of Irish Gaelic **Ó Donnghaile**,
descendant of **Donnghal**, itself meaning 'brown' + 'valour'.

Donnett other form of **Donat**

Donohue

Other form: **Donachie**

Irish – personal name; anglicized form of Irish Gaelic **O Donnchadha**, descendant of **Donnchadh**, itself meaning 'brown' + 'battle'.

Donovan

Other form: **O Donovan**

Irish – personal name; anglicized form of Irish Gaelic **Ó Donnabháin**, descendant of **Dondubhán**, itself meaning 'brown' + 'black'.

Doran

Irish – personal name; anglicized form of Irish Gaelic **Ó Deoradháin**, descendant of **Deoradhán**, itself meaning 'exile, stranger'.

Dorrell other form of Darell

Doubtfire

English – nickname; from Old English meaning 'extinguish' + 'fire'.

Douglas

Other form: **Douglass**

Scottish – place name; from several places, the name deriving from Scottish Gaelic meaning 'dark stream'. There were several powerful families of this name in medieval Scotland and it is the name of several aristocratic families at the present day. Kirk Douglas and his son Michael are 20th-century film actors.

Doyle

Irish – personal name; anglicized form of Irish Gaelic **Ó Dubhghaill**, descendant of **Dubhgall**, itself meaning 'black' + 'foreigner'. Sir Arthur Conan Doyle (1859–1930) was the creator of the Sherlock Holmes stories. Roddy Doyle (1958–) is an Irish novelist, winner of the 1994 Booker prize.

Drake

English

1 personal name; from an Old English name **Draca**, itself from Old English and Old Norse meaning 'snake' or 'dragon'.

2 nickname; from Middle English meaning 'male duck', referring to someone who resembled the bird in some way. Sir Francis Drake (1540–96) was an English navigator and pirate.

Draycott

English – place name; from many places in England, the name deriving from Old English meaning 'slipway' + 'cottage', usually a place where boats or their loads had to be dragged across land or uphill.

Drew
Other forms: **Drewett, Druce**
English
1 personal name; either a short form of **Andrew**, from Greek meaning 'manly', or from the Germanic name **Drogo**, possibly meaning 'ghost'.
2 nickname; from Old French meaning 'lover' or 'favourite'
3 place name; either from places in France called Dreux, after the Durocasses tribe of Gaul, or else from places in France whose names derive from 'de rieux' in Old French which means 'of, from' + 'streams'.
Irish
4 personal name; anglicized form of Irish Gaelic **Mac an Druaidh**, son of the druid.

Drewry other form of **Drury**

Driscoll
Irish – personal name; anglicized form of **Ó hEídirsceóil**, itself meaning 'descendant of the interpreter'.

Druce other form of **Drew**

Druery other form of **Drury**

Drummond
Scottish – place name; There are several places of this name in Scotland, deriving from Scottish Gaelic meaning 'ridge(s)'; the surname most probably comes from Drymen in Stirlingshire, of the same origin. Drummond is the family name of the Earls of Perth.

Drury
Other forms: **Drewry, Druery**
English – nickname; from Old French meaning 'love, friendship'.

Duckett
English
1 nickname; either from Middle English meaning 'duck' or from Old French meaning 'owl'.
2 personal name; either from a short form of an Old English name **Ducca**, or of a Middle English name **Duke.**

Duckworth
English – place name; from a place in Lancashire, the name probably deriving from an Old English name **Ducca** + 'enclosure'.

Duff

Scottish – nickname; from Scottish Gaelic meaning 'black, dark-haired'.

Duffy

Irish – personal name; anglicized form of Irish Gaelic **Ó Dubhthaigh**, descendant of **Dubhthach**, itself meaning 'black one'.

Duke

Other form: **Dukes**

English – occupational/nickname; from Old French meaning 'duke, captain of an army', referring either to a person with such status, or to his servant, or to an arrogant person.

Duncan

Scottish – personal name; from Scottish Gaelic meaning 'brown warrior'.

Dundas

Scottish – [in Scotland usually pronounced 'dun-**das**']

place name; from the lands in Midlothian, the name probably deriving from Scottish Gaelic meaning 'fort' + 'south'. The family of Dundas of Arniston was prominent in Scottish politics, notably in the person of Henry Dundas, Viscount Melville (1742–1811), who virtually ruled Scotland for 30 years.

Dunkley

English – place name; possibly from Dinckley in Lancashire, the name deriving from Celtic meaning 'fort' + 'wood' + Old English meaning 'clearing'.

Dunleavy

Irish – personal name; anglicized form of Irish Gaelic **Ó Duinnshléibhe**, descendant of **Duinnsliabh**, itself meaning 'brown' + 'mountain'.

Dunlop

Scottish – [in Scotland usually pronounced 'dun-**lop**']

place name; from the lands in Ayrshire, the name deriving from Scottish Gaelic meaning 'fort' + 'mud'. The place gave its name to a variety of Cheddar-like cheese. John Boyd Dunlop (1840–1921) made the name a household word by producing the pneumatic tyre.

Dybell other form of **Theobald**

E

Eacchus other form of **Eachus**

Eachus
Other form: **Eacchus**
English – place name; from a place in Cheshire, the name deriving from Old English meaning 'field of the house', an extension to an estate.

Eacock other form of **Eade**

Eade
Other forms: **Eacock, Eades, Eadie, Eakin, Eas(s)on, Ede(s), Ed(d)ison, Edeson, Edkins.**
1 English – personal name; from a Middle English familiar form of the female name **Edith**, itself meaning 'prosperity' + 'battle'.
2 English – personal name; from a Middle English short form of **Adam**, common in Scotland and N England.

Eagle
Other forms: **Eaglen, Egle**
English
1 nickname; from the name of the bird, referring to a sharp-eyed man.
2 place name; from a place in Lincolnshire of uncertain origin.

Eagles
Other form: **Egles**
English
1 nickname; other form of **Eagle.**
2 place name; from French meaning 'church',

Eakin other form of **Eade**

Ealey other form of **Ely**

Eame
Other form: **Eames**
English – nickname; from a Middle English word meaning 'uncle'. The name was probably given to someone who looked after a niece or nephew after their parents' death.

Eardley
English – place name; from a place in Staffordshire, the name deriving

from Old English meaning 'dwelling-place' + 'clearing'. Joan Eardley (1921–63) was an English painter.

Earl
Other forms: **Earle**, **Hurle.**
English
1 occupational; from Old English meaning 'nobleman', referring to a person employed in a noble household.
2 nickname; from Old English meaning 'nobleman' referring to a swaggering or snobbish person.

Earnshaw
English – place name; from a place in Lancashire, the name deriving from Old English meaning 'eagle' + 'nook, recess'.

Eason, **Easson** other forms of **Eade**

East
Other forms: **Eastes**, **Easter**, **Eastman**
English – place name; from Middle English meaning 'eastern', indicating a place to the east of the main settlement.

Eastwood
English – place name; from places in Essex and Nottingham, the former name deriving from Old English meaning 'eastern wood'; the latter derives from Old Norse meaning 'eastern clearing or enclosure'. Clint Eastwood (1930–) is an American film actor and director.

Eaton
English – place name; from many places, the name deriving from Old English meaning 'river' or 'island' + 'settlement'.

Eaves
Other forms: **Eves**, **Eavis**
English – place name; from Old English meaning 'rim, outskirts, border'.

Ebbetts
English – personal name; meaning 'son of **Isabel**'.

Eccles
English and Scottish – place name; from many places, the name deriving from Old Welsh meaning 'church'.

Eccleston
English – place name; from places in Lancashire and Cheshire, the name deriving from Old Welsh meaning 'church' + Old English meaning 'settlement'.

Eckersley
English – place name; from a place in Lancashire, the name deriving from an Old English name **Ecgeard** +'clearing'.

Eddison other form of **Eade**

Eddow, **Eddow(e)s**, other forms of **Beddows**

Ede other form of **Eade**

Eden
English
1 personal name; from a medieval name **Edun**, itself from Old English meaning 'prosperity' + 'bear cub'.
2 place name; from places in Durham, the name deriving from an Old Welsh river name meaning 'water'.

Edes other form of **Eade**

Edeson other form of **Eade**

Edess other form of **Beddow**

Edgar
Other forms: **Eggar**, **Adair**, **Agar**
English – personal name; from the first name, itself from Old English meaning 'happiness or prosperity' + 'war'.

Edge
English – place name; from Old English meaning 'ridge (of a hill), edge.'

Edgerton other form of **Egerton**

Edison other form of **Eade**

Edkins other form of **Eade**

Edmond
English – personal name; from Old English meaning 'happiness, prosperity' + 'protector'.

Edrich
Other forms: **Edridge**, **Etheridge**
English – personal name; from a medieval name meaning 'prosperity' + 'power'. William John Edrich (1916–86) was an English cricketer; as a batsman he played 39 Tests.

Edward
English – personal name; from a medieval name from Old English meaning 'prosperity, happiness' + 'guard'.

Egerton
Other forms: **Edgerton**, **Eggerton**
English – place name; from places in Cheshire and Kent, the names deriving either from Old English meaning 'settlement of **Ecgheard**' or 'settlement of **Ecghere**'. Francis Egerton, 3rd Duke of Bridgewater (1736–1803), constructed the Bridgewater Canal, the earliest canal in England, and thus became known as the 'father of British inland navigation'.

Eggar other form of **Edgar**

Egle other form of **Eagle**

Egles other form of **Eagles**

Elder
English – nickname; from Old English meaning 'elder', referring to the older one of two bearers of the same name.

Eley other form of **Ely**

Elfick other form of **Elphick**

Elford
English – place name; from places in Northumbria and Staffordshire, the name deriving from an Old English name **Ella** + 'ford', or else from 'alder tree' + 'ford'.

Elgar other form of **Alger**

Elias other form of **Ellis**

Eliot other form of **Elliot**

Elkin short form of **Elias**

Elkington
English – place name; from a place in Lincolnshire, the name probably deriving from an Old English name **Eanlac** + 'enclosure'.

Ellington
English – place name; from places in Hampshire, Northumberland and Norfolk, the name deriving from an Old English name **Ella** + 'settlement'. Duke Ellington (1899–1974) was an American pianist, composer and bandleader.

Elliot
Other forms: **Eliot**, **Elliott**
1 English – personal name; other form of **Ellis.**
2 English and Scottish – personal name; from an Old English name **Elyat** or **Elyt** which is a fusion of at least two other names. Thomas

Stearns Eliot (1888–1965) was an American-born English poet, critic and dramatist. George Eliot was the pen-name of Mary Ann Evans (1819–80), English novelist.

Ellis
Other forms: **Elias**, **Elkin**, **Elliot**, **Ellison**, **Bellis**, **Bliss** (Welsh)
1 English – personal name; short form of the medieval name **Elijah**, itself from Hebrew meaning 'Jehovah is God'.
2 English and Scottish – personal name; from a confusion of Old English names meaning 'noble' + 'battle', sometimes with the addition of the name of the Geat tribe. William Webb Ellis (1805–72) invented the game of Rugby football.

Elphick
Other forms: **Elfick**, **Elvidge**
English – personal name; from a Middle English name **Elfegh**, itself from Old English meaning 'elf' + 'high'.

Elphinstone
Other form: **Elphinston**
Scottish – place name; from the place in East Lothian, itself from a personal name + Old English meaning 'settlement.' William Elphinstone (1431–1514), from a northern branch of the family, was bishop of Aberdeen and founder of its university.

Elton
English – place name; from many places, the name deriving from an Old English name **Ella** + 'settlement'. Ben Elton is a 20th-century comic writer and performer.

Elvey
English – personal name; from Old English meaning 'elf gift'.

Elvidge other form of **Elphick**

Elvin
English – personal name; from Old English meaning 'noble' or 'elf friend'.

Elwell
English – place name; from a place in Dorset, the name deriving from Old English meaning 'omen' + 'spring'.

Elwes
English – personal name; from an Old French name **Eloise**, itself meaning 'healthy' + 'wide'.

Elwood

English – place name; from Old English meaning 'elder' + 'wood'.

Ely

Other forms: **Ealey**, **Eley**

English – place name; from the cathedral city in the Fen district, the name deriving from Old English meaning 'eel district'.

Embleton

English – place name; from several places, the name deriving from various sources, the place in Durham from Old English meaning 'elm' + 'valley', the one in Cumbria from an Old English name **Eanbald** + 'settlement'.

Embling other form of **Emmett**

Embury other form of **Amery**

Emery other form of **Amery**

Emmett

Other forms: **Embling**, **Emms**, **Em(p)son**

personal name; from a familiar form of the female name **Emma**, itself from Germanic meaning 'whole' or 'universal'.

Endacott other form of **Endecott**

Endecott

Other forms: **Endacott**, **Endicott**

English – place name; from Devon and other places, the name deriving from Middle English meaning 'end' + 'cottage'.

Enderby

English – place name; from a place in Yorkshire, the name deriving from an Old Norse name **Eindrithi** meaning 'sole ruler' + 'farm, settlement'.

Endicott other form of **Endecott**

Enfield

English – place name; from the place in Middlesex, the name deriving from Old English meaning 'lambs' + 'open country'.

Enright

Irish – personal name; anglicized form of Irish Gaelic **Mac Ionnrachtaigh**, itself meaning 'unlawful'.

Epps other forms of **Apps**

Erskine
Scottish – place name; from the lands in Renfrewshire, of doubtful origin. It is the name of several Scottish noble and landed families.

Esherwood other form of **Isherwood**

Espley
English – place name; from a place in Northumberland, the name deriving from Old English meaning 'aspen' + 'wood'.

Etchells
English – place name; from several places in N England, the name deriving from Old English meaning 'piece of land added to an estate'.

Etheridge other form of **Edrich**

Euden
English – place name; from places in Durham and Northumberland, the name deriving from Old English meaning 'yew' + 'valley'.

Evans
Welsh – personal name; from a Welsh name **Ieuan**, itself a form of **John.**

Everard
Other form: **Everett**
English – personal name; from Germanic meaning 'wild boar' + 'brave'.

Everill
English – personal name; from an Old English female name **Eoforhild** meaning 'wild boar' + 'battle'

Eves other form of **Eaves**

Ewart
English and Scottish – place name; from a place in Northumberland, the name deriving from Old English meaning 'river' +'enclosure'.

Ewbank
English – place name; from Old English meaning 'ewes' + 'hillside'.

Ewer
English – occupational; from Old French meaning 'water bearer', referring to a servant who provided water for guests to wash in between courses at meals.

Eyre other form of **Ayer**

F

Faber
English – occupational; from Latin meaning 'smith or worker in metal',

Fabian
English – personal name; from a name popular in the Middle Ages and derived from Latin **Fabianus**, itself possibly from Latin meaning 'bean'.

Fagan
Irish – personal name; anglicized form of Irish Gaelic **Ó Faodhagáin**, of uncertain origin and meaning. It may be of Norman origin.

Faherty
Irish – personal name; anglicized form of Irish Gaelic **Ó Fathartaigh**, from a personal name of uncertain meaning.

Fahy
Irish – personal name; anglicized form of Irish Gaelic **Ó Fathaigh**, probably meaning 'base, foundation'.

Fair
Other forms: **Faire, Fayre, Fayer, Feyer, Phair, Phayre**
English – nickname; from Old English meaning 'beautiful'.

Fairbairn
Scottish and N English – nickname; probably simply describing a 'fair-haired child', but it has also been suggested that it is a variant of 'freeborn'.

Fairbank
Other form: **Fairbanks**
English – place name; from Old English meaning 'lovely hillside'.

Fairbourn, Fairbourne other forms of Fairburn

Fairbrother
Other forms: **Far(e)brother, Fayerbrother**
English – nickname; from Old English meaning 'brother of a handsome person', possibly also from words meaning 'father's brother'.

Fairburn
Other form: **Fairbourn(e)**
English – place name; found in Kent and Cleveland, from Old English meaning 'fern' + 'stream'.

Faircliff, Faircliffe other forms of **Fairclough**

Faircloth other form of **Fairclough**

Fairclough
Other forms: **Faircliff, Faircliffe, Faircloth, Fairtlough, Featley**
English – place name; from Old English meaning 'fair' + 'ravine'.

Faire other form of **Fair**

Fairest other form of **Fairhurst**

Fairfax
English – nickname; from Old English meaning 'lovely' + 'hair'.

Fairfield
English – place name; from places in Derbyshire and Worcestershire, the former deriving from Old English meaning 'beautiful field', the latter from Old English meaning 'pig field'.

Fairgrieve
Scottish – nickname/occupational; The origin of the name is doubtful, including the suggestion that it is simply a combination of 'fair' + 'grieve' (a farm manager).

Fairhurst
Other form: **Fairest**
English – place name; from a hamlet near Wigan, itself from Old English meaning 'lovely' + 'wooded hill'.

Fairley other form of **Fairlie**

Fairlie
Other form: **Fairley**
Scottish – place name; from the town in Ayrshire, the name deriving from Old English meaning 'beautiful' + 'wood, clearing'.

Fairtlough other form of **Fairclough**

Fairweather
Other form: **Far(e)weather**
English and Scottish – nickname; possibly applied originally to someone who used this as a greeting, or, it is claimed, to a Scottish family emigrating to England who compared themselves to the 'fair weather (that) cometh out of the north' according to the Book of Job 37:22.

Faithful
Other form: **Faithfull**
English – nickname; from Old English and Old French meaning 'devout, loyal'.

Falcon
English – occupational/nickname; from Middle English meaning 'falcon', either referring to the job of falconer or to someone who resembled a falcon.

Falconar other form of **Falconer**

Falconer
Other forms: **Falconar**, **Falkiner**, **Falkner**, **Faulconer**, **Faulkener**, **Faulkner**, **Fawkner**
English – occupational; from Middle English meaning 'person who trained and looked after falcons'.

Fallon
Irish – personal name; anglicized form of Irish Gaelic **O Fallamhain**, 'descendant of **Fallamhan**', itself possibly meaning 'ruler'.

Fallow
Other form: **Fallow(e)s**
English – place name; from Middle English meaning 'a patch of fallow land'.

Fann, **Fanner** other forms of **Fenn**

Fanshaw, **Fanshawe** other forms of **Featherstonehaugh**

Fant
Other form: **Faunt**
English – nickname; from Old French meaning 'child'.

Faraday other form of **Fereday**

Farbrother, **Farebrother** other forms of **Fairbrother**

Farendon other form of **Farrington**

Fareweather other form of **Fairweather**

Farman
English – occupational; from an Old Norse first name meaning 'to go' + 'man' and from the name for a pedlar, itself from the Old Norse elements above.

Farmar other form of **Farmer**

Farmborough other form of **Farnborough**

Farmer
Other forms: **Farmar**, **Fermer**, **Fermor**
English – occupational; from Old French meaning 'tax collector or steward'.

Farnall other form of **Farnell**

Farnborough
Other form: **Farmborough**
English – place name; in many areas, from Old English meaning 'fern' +' mound'.

Farndon
English – place name; from Old English meaning 'fern' + 'hill'.

Farnell
Other forms: **Farnall**, **Farn(h)ill**, **Fearnall**
English – place name; from Old English, meaning 'fern' + 'hill'.

Farquhar
Other form: **Farquharson**
Scottish [pronounced **far**-kher]
personal name; from Scottish Gaelic meaning 'dear man' or 'friendly'.

Farr
English – nickname; for a strong fierce person from Old English meaning 'bull'.

Farra, **Farrah** other forms of **Farrar**

Farran, **Farrand** other form of **Farrant**

Farrant
Other forms: **Farran**, **Farrand**, **Ferran**, **Ferrand**
English – nickname; referring to someone with grey hair, or who dressed in grey, from Old French meaning 'iron-grey'.

Farrar
Other forms: **Farrier**, **Ferrier**, **Ferrar**, **Farrer**, **Farra**, **Farrah**, **Farrow**, **Pharoah**, **Varah**, **Varrow**, **Valrow**
English – occupational; from Middle English meaning 'a worker in iron'.

Farrell
Other forms: **O Farrall**, **O Ferrell**, **Farrelly**, **O Farrelly**, **Ferrally**, **O Ferrally**
Irish – personal name; anglicized form of Irish Gaelic **Ó Fearghail**, 'descendant of **Fearghal**', itself meaning 'man' + 'valour'.

Farrer, **Farrier** other forms of **Farrar**

Farringdon other form of **Farrington**

Farrington
Other forms: **Farendon**, **Farringdon**
English – place name; from Old English meaning 'farm in the fens'.

Farrow other form of **Farrar**

Farthing
English – nickname; denoting someone who paid this amount in rent or someone who lived on a piece of land so called because it was the fourth section of a large area.

Farweather other form of **Fairweather**

Fatt
English – nickname; for a plump person from Old English meaning 'fat'.

Faucett other form of **Fawcett**

Faulconer other form of **Falconer**

Faulds
Scottish – place name; from various places in central Scotland, the name probably deriving from Older Scots meaning 'folds'.

Faulkener, **Faulkner** other forms of **Falconer**

Faunt other form of **Fant**

Fawcett
Other form: **Faucett**
English – place name; from the place in Westmorland itself from Old English meaning 'varicoloured hillside'.

Fawkner other form of **Falconer**

Fay other form of **Faye**

Faye
Other form: **Fay, Fey**
English – nickname; either for someone with magic powers, from Middle English meaning 'fairy', or for someone trustworthy from Old French meaning 'loyal'.

Fayer other form of **Fair**

Fayerbrother other form of **Fairbrother**

Fayre other form of **Fair**

Fazackerly
English – place name; from a place in Lancashire, itself from Old English meaning 'border' + 'field'.

Fearnall other form of **Farnell**

Feasey other form of **Vaisey**

Feather
English – occupational; for a dealer in feathers or down, a maker of quilts or a maker of quill pens.

Featherston other form of **Featherstone**

Featherstone
Other form: **Featherston**
English – place name; from locations in Staffordshire, Yorkshire and Northumbria, the name deriving from Old English meaning 'four stones' referring to a type of prehistoric structure consisting of three upright stones topped with a fourth stone. See also **Featherstonehaugh.**

Featherstonehaugh [pronounced **fan**-shaw]
Other forms: **Featherstonhaugh**, **Fanshaw(e)**
English – place name; from a location in Northumbria now known as **Featherstone** (see above), but it originally had the ending 'haugh' from Old English meaning 'nook, enclosure'.

Featley other form of **Fairclough**

Feeley
Other form: **Feely**
Irish – personal name; anglicized form of Irish Gaelic Ó **Fithcheallaigh**, 'descendant of **Fithcheallach**', itself meaning 'chess player'.

Feely other form of **Feeley**

Feild other form of **Field**

Feilden other form of **Field**

Felix
Other form: **Fillis**
English – personal name; from Latin **Felix**, itself meaning 'fortunate, happy'.

Fell
Other form: **Fells**
English – place name; from Northern Middle English meaning 'rock, or crag'.

Felstead

English – place name; from a place in Essex, itself from Old English meaning 'pasture' + 'open country'.

Fenemore, **Fenimore** other forms of **Finnemore**

Fenix other form of **Fenwick**

Fenn

Other forms: **Fann**, **Fanner**, **Fenner**, **Fenning**, **Vance**, **Vann**, **Venn**, **Venning**

English – place name; from Old English meaning 'marsh or fen'.

Fennell

Other forms: **Funnell**, **Fonnell**

English – occupational; from Old English meaning 'fennel', denoting a grower or seller of the herb.

Fenner other form of **Fenn**

Fennick other form of **Fenwick**

Fenning other form of **Fenn**

Fenton

Other form: **Venton**

English – place name; found in many parts of Britain from Old English meaning 'marsh' + 'settlement'.

Fenwick

Other forms: **Fennick**, **Finnick**, **Fenix**, **Phoenix**

English – place name; from Old English meaning 'marsh' + 'dairy farm'.

Fereday

Other form: **Faraday**

Irish – personal name; anglicized form of Irish Gaelic **Ó Fearadaigh**, descendant of **Fearadach**, itself meaning 'man' + 'wood'. Michael Faraday (1791–1867) was an outstanding experimental physicist, whose many inventions included the introduction of electric lights in light houses.

Fergus

Other forms: **Ferguson**, **Fergusson**

Scottish – personal name; from Gaelic meaning 'man' + 'bravery, strength'.

Fermer, **Fermor** other form of **Farmer**

Ferrally other form of **Farrell**

Ferran, **Ferrand** other forms of **Farrant**

Ferrar other form of **Farrar**

Ferrey, **Ferrie**, **Ferriman** other forms of **Ferry**

Ferrier other form of **Farrar** and **Ferry**

Ferry
Other forms: **Ferrey**, **Ferrie**, **Ferrier**, **Ferriman**, **Ferryman**
English – occupational; from Old Norse meaning 'ferry', referring to a person who ferried people across a waterway, or one who lived near a ferry. Kathleen Ferrier (1912–53) was an English singer.

Fey other form of **Faye**

Feyer other form of **Fair**

Fiddler
Other form: **Fidler**
English – occupational; meaning 'fiddle player.'

Field
Other forms: **Feild**, **Fields**, **Fielden**, **Feilden**, **Fielder**, **Fielding**, **Velden**, **Attfield**, **Delafield**
English – place name; from Old English meaning 'pasture, open country'. Henry Fielding (1707–54) was an English novelist. Gracie Fields (1898–1979) was an English singer.

Fife other form of **Fyfe**

Fillis other form of **Felix**

Findlay
Other forms: **Finlay**, **Finlayson**
Scottish – personal name; from Scottish Gaelic meaning 'fair' + 'warrior'.

Finemore other form of **Finnemore**

Finlay, **Finlayson** other forms of **Findlay**

Finnegan
Other form: **Finucane**
Irish – nickname; from Irish Gaelic **Ó Fionnagáin**, meaning 'descendant of the fair-haired one'.

Finnemore
Other forms: **Fen(n)emore**, **Fenimore**, **Finemore**
English – nickname; from Old French meaning 'fine, splendid' + 'love'.

Finney

Other form: **Finnie**

English – place name; from several places in Cheshire, probably from Old English meaning 'wood pile.'

Finnick other form of **Fenwick**

Finnie other form of **Finney**

Finucane other form of **Finnegan**

Firbank

Other form: **Furbank**

English – place name; from Middle English meaning 'woodland' + 'slope'.

Fish

Other forms: **Fisk, Fiske**

English – occupational; from Old English and Old Norse meaning 'fish', referring to someone who caught or sold fish.

Fisher

English – occupational/place name; from Old English meaning 'fisherman', or else 'fishery'.

Fisk, Fiske other forms of **Fish**

Fitzclarence

English – personal name; combining the Norman-French prefix 'Fitz' meaning 'son of' and the first name **Clarence.** The surname was initiated by George Fitzclarence, Earl of Munster (1794–1842), one of the illegitimate children of the Duke of Clarence (who became William IV) and the actress, Mrs Jordan.

Fitzgerald

Irish – personal name; combining the Norman-French prefix 'Fitz' meaning 'son of' and the first name **Gerald.** The surname was established in Ireland in the Middle Ages by the son of an English landowner whose descendants became powerful members of the Irish aristocracy. Francis Scott Key Fitzgerald (1896–1940) was an American novelist.

Fitzgibbon

English – personal name; combining the Norman-French prefix 'Fitz' meaning 'son of' and the name **Gibb**, a familiar form of **Gilbert**, itself from Norman-French of Germanic origin meaning 'pledge' + 'bright'.

Fitzherbert

English – personal name; combining the Norman-French prefix 'Fitz' meaning 'son of' and the name **Herbert**, itself from Norman-French of Germanic origin meaning 'army' + 'bright'. Maria Anne Fitzherbert (1756–1837) secretly married the Prince of Wales in 1785.

Fitzpatrick
Irish – personal name; from the first name **Patrick** and usually an anglicized form of the Irish Gaelic surname **Mac Giolla Pádraig** itself meaning 'son of the servant of **Patrick**' though it may occasionally be an original combination of the Norman-French prefix 'Fitz' meaning 'son of' and the first name **Patrick**

Fitzroy other form of **Ray**

Fitzsimmons other form of **Simon**

Fitzwilliam other form of **William**

Flanagan
Other forms: **Flanaghan, Flannagan, Flannigan**
Irish – personal name; anglicized form of Irish Gaelic **Ó Flannagáin**, 'descendant of **Flannagán**', itself from Irish Gaelic meaning 'reddish, ruddy'.

Flanner
English – occupational; from Old French meaning 'custard' or 'pancake', referring to a cook who made such dishes.

Flannigan other form of **Flanagan**

Fleming
English and Scottish – nickname; from Norman-French of Germanic origin meaning ' person from Flanders'. Ian Fleming (1908–64) was a British novelist and creator of the thriller hero, James Bond.

Fletcher
English – occupational; from Old English meaning 'maker of arrows'.

Flett
Scottish – place name/nickname; Originally an Orkney name, it may be derived from a Shetland place name (from Old Norse meaning 'a strip of arable or grass-land'), or it may be from an Old Norse nickname meaning 'swift, fast'.

Fletton
English – place name; from Old English meaning 'place on a river'.

Flewett other form of **Flewitt**

Flewitt
Other forms: **Flewett, Flowitt**

English – personal name; from a Norman French name **Flodhard**, itself from Germanic meaning 'fame' + 'brave'.

Flint

English – place name; from Old English meaning 'flint or stone', referring to someone who lived near an outcrop of this material.

Flowitt other form of **Flewitt**

Floyd other form of **Lloyd**

Foden

Other form: **Fowden**

English – place name; common in Cheshire, from Old English meaning 'colourful' + 'hollow'.

Folkes, **Folks** other forms of **Foulkes**

Fonnell other form of **Fennell**

Fooks other form of **Foulkes**

Foot

Other forms: **Foote**, **Footitt**

English – nickname; from Middle English meaing 'foot', referring to someone with distinctive feet. Michael Foot (1913–) is a Labour politician and former party leader.

Forber other form of **Frobisher**

Forbes

Scottish – place name; from the lands in Aberdeenhire, probably from old Gaelic meaning 'at the land or district'. It was the name of several landowning families in NE Scotland. Duncan Forbes of Culloden was an 18th-century judge who played a prominent role in Scottish politics during the Jacobite risings of 1715 and 1745.

Ford

Other forms: **Forde**, **Forder**

English – place name; from numerous places, the name deriving from Old English meaning 'ford'. Henry Ford (1863–1947) was an American automobile engineer and manufacturer.

Fordyce

Scottish – place name; from the lands in Banffshire, the name deriving from Old Gaelic meaning 'slope' + 'south'.

Forest

Other forms: **Forrest**, **For(r)ester**, **Forster**

English – occupational; from Old French meaning 'forest', referring to someone who worked in forestry or gamekeeping. E M Forster (1879–1970) was an English novelist and critic.

Forsyth
Other form: **Forsythe**
Scottish [pronounced for-**scythe**]
personal name/place name; either from an Old Gaelic name meaning 'man' + 'peace' or from a place name (unidentified). Although Scottish in origin, the name has several well-known English bearers, including the entertainer Bruce Forsyth (1928–), the author Frederick Forsyth (1938–), as well as the 18th-century botanist who gave his name to the shrub forsythia.

Fortescue
Other form: **Fortesquieu**
English – nickname; from Old French meaning 'strong shield'.

Foster
English
1 nickname; from Old English meaning 'fostered', referring to a foster-child or foster-parent.
2 occupational; from Middle English meaning 'forester, gamekeeper'. Sir Norman Foster (1935–) is an English architect.

Foulkes
Other forms: **Folk(e)s, Fooks, Fowkes, Vokes, Volk(e)s**
English – personal name; from several Germanic names containing an element meaning 'folk'.

Fowden other form of **Foden**

Fowkes other form of **Foulkes**

Fowler
English – occupational; from Old English meaning 'bird catcher'.

Frain other form of **Frayn**

Fraser
Other form: **Frazer**
Scottish – Of unknown origin; early forms suggest a Norman-French connection and the name has been associated with the Old French word for the strawberry plant (which features in the family coat-of-arms). The Frasers held land in several parts of Scotland, including the north where they became a Highland clan with Lord Lovat as their head.

Frayn
Other form: **Frain**

English – place name; from Old French meaning 'ash tree'. Michael Frayn (1933–) is an English dramatist.

Frazer other form of **Fraser**

Frederick
English – personal name; from Germanic meaning 'peace + power' and introduced into England by the Normans.

Free
Other forms: **Freebody**, **Freeman**
English – nickname; from Old English meaning 'free-born', referring to the status of someone who was not a serf. See also **Freedman**.

Freedman
English – nickname; from Old English meaning 'liberated serf'. Although the name is more commonly Jewish, from Yiddish meaning 'peace', it exists as an English surname in Yorkshire. See also **Free.**

Freeman other form of **Free**

French
English – nickname; for someone from France or for someone with French mannerisms.

Frew
Scottish – place name; from the Fords of Frew, at one time the lowest crossing point on the River Forth. The name is of obscure origin, possibly from an Old Welsh root.

Frobisher
Other forms: **Furber**, **Forber.**
English – occupational; from Old French meaning 'furbisher, polisher of armour'.

Frodsham
Other form: **Frodson**
English – place name; from a place in Cheshire, the name deriving from Old English meaning 'homestead' + **Frod**, itself meaning 'wise'.

Fry
English – nickname; from Old English meaning 'freeborn' or 'noble, generous'. Christopher Fry (1907–) is an English dramatist.

Fullarton other form of **Fullerton**

Fuller
Other form: **Voller**
English – occupational; from Old English meaning 'fuller', that is, a

worker who thickened raw cloth by beating it in water.

Fullerton
Other form: **Fullarton**
Scottish and N Irish – place name; from places in Ayrshire and Angus, the name deriving from Old English meaning 'fowler, bird-catcher' + 'settlement'.

Fulton
Scottish and N Irish – place name; from places in Ayrshire (not now known) and Roxburghshire, the name possibly deriving from Old English meaning 'fowl' + 'settlement'.

Funnell other form of **Fennell**

Furbank other form of **Firbank**

Furber other form of **Frobisher**

Furlong
English – place name; from Middle English meaning 'furrow' + 'long', the technical term for the unit of cultivation divided into strips and worked by several people under the medieval system of farming.

Furnass other form of **Furness**

Furness
Other forms: **Furniss, Furnass**
English – place name; in Cumbria, the name deriving from Old Norse meaning 'rump' + 'nose or headland'.

Furnifall other form of **Furnival**

Furniss other form of **Furness**

Furnival
Other forms: **Furnifall, Furnivall**
English – place name; in France, the name deriving from Old French meaning 'kiln' + 'settlement'.

Fyfe
Other forms: **Fife, Fyffe**
Scottish – place name; from the county, the name deriving from one of the ancient provinces of the land of the Picts; its origin is obscure.

G

Gabriel

English – personal name; from the first name, itself from Hebrew meaning 'man of God'.

Gadd

English – occupational; from Middle English meaning 'goad, spike', referring to a cattle driver.

Gadsby

English – place name; from Gaddesby in Leicestershire, the name deriving from Old Norse from a personal name **Gaddr** meaning 'sting' + 'farm'.

Gaffney

Irish – personal name; anglicized form of Irish Gaelic **Ó Gamhna**, 'descendant of **Gamhain**', itself meaning 'calf'.

Gage

Other forms: **Ga(i)ger**, **Gauge**

English – occupational; from Middle English meaning 'measure', referring to the official in charge of checking weights and measures, an assayer.

Gail other form of **Gale**

Gain

Other form: **Gains**, **Gaines**

English – nickname; from Norman-French of Germanic origin meaning 'trickery'.

Gaitskell, **Gaitskill** other forms of **Gaskell**

Galbraith

Scottish [pronounced gal-**braith**]

nickname; from Scottish Gaelic meaning 'foreigner, stranger' + 'Briton', probably referring to one of the Britons of Strathclyde. John Kenneth Galbraith (1908–) is a well-known N American economist.

Gale

Other forms: **Gail**, **Gallon**, **Gayle**,

English

1 occupational; from Norman-French of Germanic origin meaning

'gaol', referring to a prison keeper.

2 nickname; from Old English meaning 'light, merry'.

3 personal name; from Norman-French of Germanic origin meaning 'cheerful' + 'foreigner'.

Gall
English – nickname; from Celtic meaning 'foreigner, stranger'.

Gallacher other form of **Gallagher**

Gallagher
Other forms: **Gallacher**, **Gallagher**, **Gallogher**, **O Gallagher**
Irish – personal name; anglicized form of Irish Gaelic **Ó Gallchobhair**, 'descendant of **Gallchobhair**', itself meaning 'foreign' + 'help'.

Galliford other form of **Gulliver**

Galliver other form of **Gulliver**

Gallogher other form of **Gallagher**

Gallon other form of **Gale**

Gallop
Other form: **Gallup**
English – nickname; from 'gallop' meaning 'run'. The American statistician, George Gallup, devised the Gallup Poll in 1935 to sample the views of a representative section of the community.

Galloway
Scottish – place name; from the area in SW Scotland, the name deriving from Scottish Gaelic meaning 'stranger' + 'Gael'.

Gallup other form of **Gallop**

Galsworthy
Other form: **Golsworthy**
English – place name; of a place in Devon, the name deriving from Old English meaning 'sweet gale' + 'slope'. John Galsworthy (1867–1933) was an English novelist.

Galton
English – place name; from Old English meaning 'rented farm'.

Gambell other form of **Gamble**

Gamble
Other forms: **Gambell**, **Gammell**, **Gammil**
English – personal name; from Old Norse meaning 'old'. See also **Gemmell**.

Gamidge other form of **Gammage**

Gammage
Other form: **Gam(m)idge**
English – place name; from Gamaches in northern France, itself probably from Celtic meaning 'winding' + 'water'.

Gammell, **Gammil** other forms of **Gamble**

Gandy
English – Of uncertain origin, but two possibilities are:
1 occupational; from French meaning 'glove', referring to a glove maker.
2 place name; from a place in France.

Garbett
English – personal name; from Norman-French of Germanic origin meaning 'spear' + 'bright'.

Garden other form of **Gardner**

Gardner
Other forms: **Garden**, **Gardener**, **Gardiner**, **Jardin(e)**
English – occupational; from Middle English meaning 'orchard or kitchen garden'.

Garland
English
1 occupational; referring to a maker of wreaths.
2 place name; from a place in Devon, the name deriving from Old English meaning 'triangular piece of land' + 'land'.

Garlic other form of **Garlick**

Garlick
Other form: **Garlic**
English – occupational; from Middle English meaning 'garlic', referring to a grower or seller of the plant.

Garman other form of **Gorman**

Garmondsway
English – place name; from a place in Co. Durham, the name deriving from Old English meaning 'spear protector' + 'road'.

Garner
English – occupational; from Norman-French of Germanic origin meaning 'barn, granary', referring to a keeper of the granary.

Garnett

English – occupational; from Old French meaning either 'hinge' or 'pomegranate' and referring to sellers of these.

Garrard other form of **Garrett**

Garratt other form of **Garrett**

Garrett

Other forms: **Garrard, Garratt, Gerard, Jarrard, Jarratt, Jarrett, Jerrold, Jerrott**

English – personal name; from **Gerard**. See **Gerard.**

Garside

Other form: **Gartside**

English – place name; from a place in Lancashire, the name deriving from Middle English meaning 'enclosure' + 'slope'.

Garvey other form of **Garvie**

Garvie

Other form: **Garvey**

Scottish and Irish – nickname; from Gaelic meaning 'rough', or from an Irish personal name of the same origin.

Gascogne other form of **Gascoigne**

Gascoigne

Other forms: **Gascogne, Gascon, Gascoyne, Gasken, Gaskin**

English – place name; referring to a person from Gascony in France. Paul Gascoigne is an English footballer.

Gaskell

Other forms: **Gaskill, Gaitskell, Gaitskill**

English – place name; from Gaitsgill in Cumbria, the name deriving from Old Norse meaning 'goat' + 'shelter'. Elizabeth Cleghorn Gaskell (1810–65) was an English novelist.

Gasken other form of **Gascoigne**

Gaskill other form of **Gaskell**

Gaskin other form of **Gascoigne**

Gateley

Other form: **Gatley**

English – place name; from a place in Cheshire, the name deriving from Old English meaning 'clearing' + 'goats.'

Gates
English – place name; from Old English meaning 'way or street'. Bill Gates is a 20th-century computer pioneer.

Gauge other form of **Gage**

Gavin
English – personal name; from the first name, itself probably from Old Welsh meaning 'hawk' + 'white'.

Gawkrodger other form of **Gawkroger**

Gawkroger
Other form: **Gawkrodger**
English – nickname; from a dialect word meaning 'clumsy' + **Roger**, originally referring to an inept archer.

Gay
Other form: **Gaye**
English
1 nickname; for a cheerful person.
2 place name; from Gaye in Normandy.

Gayle other form of **Gale**

Gaylord
English – nickname; from Norman-French of Germanic origin meaning 'high-spirited'.

Gayton
English – place name; from Old English meaning 'goat' + 'settlement'.

Gazely
English – place name; from a place in Suffolk, the name deriving from an Old English name **Gaegi** + 'clearing'.

Gear
English – nickname; from Old Norse meaning 'trick'.

Gearing
English – nickname; from Middle English meaning 'villain' or 'glutton'.

Geaves other forms of **Jeeves**

Geddes
Scottish – place name; from the place near Nairn, itself of doubtful origin, possibly from Gaelic meaning 'meadow'. Sir Patrick Geddes (1854–1932) was a sociologist and pioneer of town planning. Jenny

Geddes (c1600-c1660) is said to have started the riots over Laud's prayer book by hurling her stool at the bishop in St Giles' Cathedral, Edinburgh.

Gee
English – personal name; of uncertain origin.

Geeves other form of **Jeeves**

Geldard
Other forms: **Geldart**, **Gelder**
English – occupational; from Old English meaning 'keeper of sterile goats'.

Gelding
English – nickname; from Old Norse meaning 'gelding, eunuch'.

Gemmel other form of **Gemmell**

Gemmell
Other forms: **Gemmel**, **Gemmill**
Scottish – personal name; from Old Norse meaning 'old one'. See also **Gamble.**

Genner other form of **Jenner**

Genower other form of **Jenner**

Gent other form of **Gentle**

Gentile other form of **Gentle**

Gentle
Other forms: **Gent**, **Gentile**, **Gentry**, **Jent**, **Jentle**,
English – nickname; from Middle English meaning 'noble' or 'courteous'.

Geoffrey other form of **Jeffrey**

George
English – personal name; from Old French, through Latin from Greek meaning 'farmer'.

Gerald
English – personal name; from Norman-French of Germanic origin meaning 'spear' + 'rule'.

Gerard
Other form: **Gerrard**
English – personal name; from Norman-French of Germanic origin meaning 'spear' + 'strong'. See also **Garrett.**

Gervase, **Gervis** other forms of **Jarvis**

Gibb

Other forms: **Gibbs**, **Gibbon**, **Gibbons**

Scottish and English – personal name; from an old familiar form of **Gilbert.** Edward Gibbon (1737–94) was an English historian.

Gibson

Scottish – personal name; meaning 'son of **Gilbert**'.

Giffard other form of **Gifford**

Gifford

Other form: **Giffard**

English – nickname; from Norman-French of Germanic origin meaning 'chubby, puffy-cheeked'.

Gilbert

English – personal name; from Norman-French of Germanic origin meaning 'pledge' + 'bright'.

Gilbey other form of **Gilby**

Gilby

Other form: **Gilbey**

English – place name; from a place in Lincolnshire, the name deriving from an Old Norse name **Gilli** + 'settlement'.

Gilchrist

Scottish – personal name; from a Scottish Gaelic personal name, once common in the Highlands, meaning 'servant of Christ'.

Giles

English – personal name; from Latin **Aegidius**, itself from Greek meaning 'young goat'.

Gilfillan

Scottish – personal name; from a Scottish Gaelic name, meaning 'servant of St Fillan'.

Gilham other form of **William**

Gilkes

English – personal name; meaning 'son of **William**'.

Gillam

Other form: **Gillem**

English – personal name; from the English spelling of the French form of **William.**

Gillatt other form of **Gillett**

Gillespie
Scottish – personal name; from a Scottish Gaelic name meaning 'servant of the bishop'. Dizzy Gillespie (1917–) is a pioneering jazz musician.

Gillett
Other forms: **Gill(i)att, Gilliot, Gillot, Gillyatt, Jellett, Jillett, Jellitt**
English
1 personal name; from diminutives of **Giles, Julian** or **William.**
2 place name; from Middle English meaning 'ravine' + 'head'.

Gilliam other form of **William**

Gilliatt other form of **Gillett**

Gillies
Scottish – personal name; from a Scottish Gaelic name meaning 'servant of Jesus'.

Gillingham
English – place name; from places in Dorset and Kent, the name deriving from Old English meaning 'homestead of **Gythla**', a personal name meaning 'battle'.

Gilliot other form of **Gillett**

Gillot other form of **Gillett**

Gillow
English – place name; from a place in Herefordshire, the name deriving from Welsh meaning 'retreat' + 'pool'.

Gillyatt other form of **Gillett**

Gilmore other form of **Gilmour**

Gilmour
Other form: **Gilmore**
Scottish – personal name; from a Scottish Gaelic name, meaning 'servant of the Virgin Mary'.

Gilroy
Other form of **Kilroy**
Irish – personal name from Irish Gaelic **Mac Giolla Ruaidh**, itself meaning 'son of the red-haired lad'.

Ginner other form of **Jenner**

Girton
English – place name; from Old English meaning 'gravel' + 'settlement'.

Gladstone
Scottish – place name; formerly Gledstane(s) in Lanarkshire, the name deriving from a farm name, itself from Old English meaning 'kite, hawk' + 'stone'. The British prime minister, William Ewart Gladstone (1809–98) was born in Liverpool of Scottish parents.

Gladwin
English – nickname; from Old English meaning 'glad' + 'friend'.

Glaisher
English – occupational; from Old English meaning 'glazier'.

Glancy other form of **Clancy**

Glandfield, Glanfield other forms of **Glanville**

Glanvill other form of **Glanville**

Glanville
Other forms: **Glanvill, Glan(d)field**
English – place name; either from a place in Calvados, itself from a Norman-French personal name of Germanic origin + 'settlement', or from place names in England (such as Clanville in Somerset or Clanfield in Hampshire) from Old English meaning 'clean' + 'field'.

Glasgow
Scottish – place name; from the city name, itself probably from Old Welsh meaning 'grey-green' + 'hollows'.

Glass
1 English – occupational; from Old English meaning 'glass', referring to a glazier or glassblower.
2 Scottish and Irish – nickname; from Gaelic meaning 'grey'.

Glassbrook other form of **Glazebrook**

Glasscock other form of **Glasscott**

Glasscote other form of **Glasscott**

Glasscott
Other forms: **Glasscock, Glasscote**
English – occupational; from Old English 'glass' + 'hut', referring to a glassblower.

Glave other form of **Gleave**

Glazebrook
Other form: **Glassbrook**
English – place name; from a place in Lancashire which stands on the Glaze Brook.

Gleave
Other form: **Gleaves, Glave**
English – occupational; from Middle English meaning 'sword',
referring to a maker or seller of swords, or to a skilled swordsman.

Glen
Other form: **Glenn**
Scottish – place name; from Scottish Gaelic meaning '(narrow)
valley'. Many families of the name are thought to descend from a
family from Glen near Peebles.

Glendenning other form of **Glendinning**

Glendinning
Other form: **Glendenning**
Scottish – place name; from the lands in Dumfries-shire, the name
probably deriving from Old Welsh meaning 'valley' + 'fort' + 'white'.

Glenn other form of **Glen**

Glennie
Other form: **Glenny**
Scottish – place name; from several places in NE Scotland, the name
probably deriving from Scottish Gaelic meaning 'narrow valley'.
Evelyn Glennie is a successful 20th-century percussion player.

Glover
English – occupational; from Middle English referring to a maker or
seller of gloves.

Gobert other form of **Godbert**

Godard, Godart other forms of **Goddard**

Godber other form of **Godbert**

Godbert
Other forms: **Gobert, Godber**
English – personal name; from the medieval name **Godebert**, itself
from Old English meaning 'good' + 'bright'.

Goddard
Other forms: **Godard, Godart**
English – personal name; from Norman-French of Germanic origin,
meaning 'good' + 'brave'.

Godfrey
English – personal name; from Norman-French of Germanic origin
meaning 'God' + 'peace'.

Godley
Other forms: **Godly, Goodl(e)y, Goodleigh**
English – place name; from places in Devon and Cheshire, the name deriving from an Old English name '**Goda**' + 'wood, clearing'.

Godman other form of **Goodman**

Godwin
Other form: **Goodwin**
English – personal name; from Old English meaning 'God' + 'friend'.

Goff, Goffe other forms of **Gough**

Gold other form of **Gould**

Goldie
Other forms: **Goudie, Goudy, Gowdie.**
Scottish – nickname; a diminutive of **Gold**, it was sometimes given as a nickname to the treasurer of a trade in a town.

Golding
English – personal name; from an Old English name meaning 'gold'.

Goldsmith
English – occupational; from Old English meaning 'gold' + 'metal worker'.

Golsworthy other form of **Galsworthy**

Gomer
Other form: **Gummer**
English – personal name; from a Middle English name **Godmer**, itself from Germanic meaning 'good' + 'famous'.

Gooch other form of **Gough**

Goodall
Other form: **Goodhall**
English
1 place name; from places in Yorkshire from Old English meaning 'marigold' + 'nook, recess'.
2 occupational; from Middle English meaning 'good' + 'ale'. Jane Goodall's pioneering research on gorillas has been influential in the late 20th century.

Goodbaudy other form of **Goodbody**

Goodbody
Other form: **Goodbaudy**
English – nickname; from Middle English meaning 'good' + 'creature'.

Goodge other form of **Gough**

Goodger other form of **Goodyear**

Goodhall other form of **Goodall**

Goodier other form of **Goodyear**

Goodlad

Scottish – nickname; probably for a reliable servant. The name is still common in the Shetland Islands. Sir Alistair Goodlad is a Conservative politician.

Goodleigh, **Goodley**, **Goodly** other forms of **Godley**

Goodman

Other form: **Godman**

English

1 personal name; from Middle English **Godeman**, meaning 'good man'.

2 occupational; from 'good' and 'man' functioning as the title for a householder.

Goodrich other form of **Gutteridge**

Goodridge other form of **Gutteridge**

Goodwin other form of **Godwin**

Goodyear

Other forms: **Goodger**, **Goodier**, **Goodyer**, **Gudger**

English – nickname; from Middle English 'good' + 'year'.

Gordon

Scottish – place name; from a place in Berwickshire, possibly deriving from Old Welsh meaning 'spacious' + 'fort'. There have long been important branches of the family in NE Scotland and it is the family name of the Marquess of Aberdeen and the Marquess of Huntly. Lord Byron was George Gordon (from his mother's name).

Gore

English – place name; from Old English meaning 'triangular plot of ground'.

Goreham

English – place name; from Old English meaning 'triangular plot of ground' + 'homestead'.

Gorman

Other form: **Garman**

English

1 personal name; from a Middle English name **Gormund** meaning 'spear' + 'protection'.
2 place name; from Old English meaning 'triangular plot of ground' + 'man'.

Gormilly other form of **Gormley**

Gormley
Other forms: **Gormilly, Grumly**
Irish – personal name; anglicized form of Irish Gaelic **Ó Gormghaile**, 'descendant of **Gormghal**', itself meaning 'noble' + 'valour'.

Goseling other form of **Gosling**

Gosland other form of **Gosling**

Gosling
Other forms: **Goseling, Gosland, Gostling,**
1 nickname; from Middle English meaning 'gosling'.
2 personal name; other form of **Joscelyn**.

Gossard
Other form: **Gossart**
English – occupational; from Middle English meaning 'goose herd'.

Gosse
English – personal name; from **Gosse**, a name deriving from Norman-French of Germanic origin, meaning 'good'.

Gostling other form of **Gosling**

Goudie, Goudy other forms of **Goldie**

Gough
Other forms: **Goff(e), Gooch, Goodge, Gudge, Gutch**
English and Welsh
1 occupational; from Gaelic meaning 'smith'. See also **Gow.**
2 nickname; from Welsh meaning 'red', referring to a red-haired person.

Gould
Other form: **Gold**
English – personal name; from an Old English name meaning 'golden-haired, rich'.

Gourlay
Other forms: **Gourley, Gourlie**
Scottish – place name; of obscure origin, possibly from a place in Normandy.

Govan

Scottish – place name; from the place in Lanarkshire (now part of Glasgow).

Gow

Scottish – occupational; from Gaelic meaning 'smith'. Niel Gow (1727–1807) was an outstanding Scottish fiddle-player. See also **Gough.**

Gowdie other form of **Goldie**

Grace

English

1 nickname; from Middle English meaning 'grace, pleasantness'.
2 personal name; from the female name **Grace**, itself from a Germanic element meaning 'grey', but popularly associated with 'grace'. W G Grace (1848–1915) was an English cricketer.

Grady

Other form: **O Grady**

Irish – personal name; anglicized form of Irish Gaelic **Ó Gráda**, 'descendant of **Gráda**', itself meaning 'noble'.

Graeme other form of **Graham**

Grafton

English – place name; from Old English meaning 'grove' + 'settlement'.

Graham

Other forms: **Grahame, Graeme**

Scottish – place name; from an English manor, the name deriving from Old English meaning 'grey' + 'home'. Of Norman-French origin, the Grahams held power in central and S Scotland. Billy Graham (1918–) is an American evangelist. Kenneth Grahame (1859–1932) was a Scottish writer and author of *Wind in the Willows.*

Grainger

Other forms: **Grange, Granger**

English – occupational; from Middle English 'granary' referring to a farm bailiff with responsibility for the collection of grain and other contributions due to a landlord.

Grant

Scottish – nickname; from French meaning 'great'. Of Norman-French origin, the Grants became a powerful clan with lands in NE Scotland.

Gratorex, Gratrix other forms of **Greatrakes**

Grattan other form of **Gratton**

Gratten other form of **Gratton**

Gratton
Other forms: **Grattan, Gratten**
English – place name; from Old English meaning 'large' + 'enclosure'.

Gray
Other form: **Grey**
English – nickname; for a person with grey hair.

Greatrakes
Other forms: **Gratorex, Gratrix, Greatrex**
English – place name; from Old English meaning 'big' + 'path'. In Derbyshire mining areas it was used to refer to 'a vein of ore' and this is probably the origin of the place known as Great Rocks near Wormhill in Derbyshire.

Greave
Other forms: **Greaves, Greve**
English – place name; from Old English meaning 'thicket'.

Green other form of **Greene**

Greene
Other form: **Green**
English – place name; from Old English meaning 'green', referring to a village green. Graham Greene (1904–91) was an English novelist.

Greenlee, Greenlees, Greenley other forms of **Grindley**

Greer other form of **Grier.**

Greg, Gregg other forms of **Greig**

Gregor other form of **Gregory**

Gregory
Other forms: **Gregor, Grigor** (Scottish)
English – personal name; from the first name, itself from Greek meaning 'watchful'.

Greig
Other forms: **Greg, Gregg, Grieg**
Scottish – personal name; from **Gregory**, but also influenced by the name of one of the Pictish kings. The Norwegian composer Edvard Grieg (1843–1907) was descended from an Aberdeenshire family.

Gresham
English – place name; from a place in Norfolk, meaning 'pasture land' + 'homestead'.

Gresty
English – place name; from a place in Cheshire, from Old English meaning 'badger run'.

Greve other form of **Greave**

Grew
Other forms: **Grewcock**, **Grocock**, **Grocott**
English – nickname; for a tall skinny person, from Middle English meaning 'crane'.

Grey other form of **Gray**

Grice
Other forms: **Grise**, **Griss**
English
1 nickname; from Middle English meaning 'grey', referring to a person with grey hair.
2 occupational; from Middle English meaning 'pig', referring to the job of swineherd.

Grieg other form of **Greig**

Grier
Other forms: **Greer**, **Grierson**
Scottish – personal name; probably from **Gregory.** Germaine Greer (1939–) is an Australian writer and feminist.

Grieve
Scottish – occupational; from Scots meaning 'overseer, steward, farm bailiff'.

Griffin other form of **Griffith**

Griffith
Other form: **Griffiths**, **Griffin**
Welsh – personal name; from an Old Welsh name **Gruffydd**, the ending of which means 'chief', the first part being of uncertain origin.

Grigor Scottish form of **Gregor**

Grime other form of **Grimes**

Grimes
Other form: **Grime**
English – personal name; from Old Norse **Grimr**, meaning 'masked person'.

Grimshaw
English – place name; from places in Lancashire, the name deriving from Old Norse meaning 'masked person' + 'copse'.

Grindley
Other forms: **Greenley**, **Greenlee(s)**, **Grinley**
English – place name; from many places, the name deriving from Old English meaning 'green' + 'clearing, wood'.

Grise other form of **Grice**

Grisedale
Other form: **Grisdale**
English – place name; from Old Norse meaning 'pig' + valley'.

Grisewood
English – place name; from Old Norse and Old English, meaning 'pig' + 'wood'.

Griss other form of **Grice**

Grocock other form of **Grew**

Grocott other form of **Grew**

Grumly other form of **Gormley**

Gudge other form of **Gough**

Gudger other form of **Goodyear**

Gulliford other form of **Gulliver**

Gulliver
Other forms: **Gulliford**, **Galliford**, **Galliver**
English – nickname; for a glutton, from Norman-French of Germanic origin.

Gummer other form of **Gomer**

Gunn
Scots and English – personal name; from a shortened form of various Old Norse names beginning with this element (meaning 'battle'). Though Norse in origin, the family became a Highland clan based in the far north of Scotland. Neil M Gunn (1891–1973) was a well-known novelist.

Gunnell other form of **Connell**

Gunter
English – personal name; from a Norman-French name of Germanic origin meaning 'battle' + 'army'.

Guppy

Other form: **Guppie**

English – place name; from a place in Dorset, the name deriving from Old English, meaning 'battle' + 'famous' + 'enclosure'.

Gutch other form of **Gough**

Guthrie

Scottish – place name; from the place in Angus, the name possibly deriving from Scottish Gaelic meaning 'windy place'.

Gutteridge

Other forms: **Goodrich**, **Goodridge**, **Gut(t)ridge**,

English – personal name; from Middle English from either of two names, **Goderiche**, meaning 'good' + 'power', or else **Cuterich**, meaning 'well-known' + 'power'.

Guy

English – personal name; from a Norman-French name **Wido** of Germanic origin, possibly meaning 'wood'.

H

Habersham
Other forms: **Habershon**, **Haversham**, **Havisham**
English – occupational; from Middle English meaning 'mail jerkin', referring to a maker of garments of chain mail.

Hackett
Other forms: **Haggett**, **Haggit**
English – personal name; from a medieval name **Hake**, itself from Old Norse meaning 'hook'.

Hadaway other form of **Hathaway**

Hadden other form of **Howden**

Haddock
English – Of uncertain origin, but the following are possible:
1 occupational; from Middle English meaning 'haddock', referring to a fishmonger.
2 personal name; from an Old English name **Aeduc**, the first part meaning prosperity.
3 place name; from Haydock near Liverpool, the name deriving from Old English meaning 'heath' + 'hook'.

Haddon
English – place name; from places in Derbyshire, Dorset and Northants, from Old English meaning 'heathland' + 'hill'.

Haddow
Scottish – place name; may be a contraction of **Haddock**, or possibly from Haddo in Aberdeenshire, the name deriving from an old Scottish land measure.

Hadfield other form of **Hatfield**

Hadleigh other form of **Hadley**

Hadley
Other forms: **Hadleigh**, **Headley**
English – place name; from many places, the name usually deriving from Old English meaning 'heathland' + 'clearing', apart from one from Worcestershire deriving from an Old English name **Hadda**, meaning 'brave' + 'clearing'.

Haggett, **Haggitt** other forms of **Hackett**

Hague other form of **Haig**

Haig
Other forms: **Haigh**, **Hague**
1 Scottish – place name; from a Normandy place name, itself derived from Old Norse meaning 'enclosure'. The family owned the estates of Bemersyde on the Tweed from medieval times until 1867, and after World War I they were bought back by a grateful nation for Field Marshal Douglas Haig, who became 1st Earl Haig.
2 English – place name; from Old English meaning 'enclosure'.

Haighton
English – place name; from a place in Lancashire, the name deriving from Old English meaning 'place in a nook or recess' + 'settlement'.

Haile, **Hailes** other forms of **Hale**

Hailey other form of **Haley**

Haime other form of **Hammond**

Hain
Other forms: **Hayn**, **Hayne**
English
1 place name; from Old English meaning 'fences, enclosures'.
2 personal name; from the Middle English personal name **Hain** or **Heyne**.
3 nickname; for a poor, wretched person from Middle English meaning 'wretch'.

Halcro other form of **Halcrow**

Halcrow
Other form: **Halcro**
Scottish – place name; from the lands on the Orkney island of South Ronaldsay, the name deriving from Old Norse, possibly meaning 'high enclosure'.

Haldane
Scottish
1 personal name; from an Old English personal name (based on Old Norse) meaning 'half-Dane'.
2 place name; other form of **Howden**. The Haldane family have held land in Perthshire since the 13th century. Famous bearers of the name include R B Haldane (1856–1928), Scottish judge and politician, and his nephew the biologist J B S Haldane (1892–1964).

Hale

Other forms: **Haile(s)**, **Heal(e)**, **Hele**, **Haugh**

English

1 place name; from Old English meaning 'nook, recess'.

2 personal name; from Middle English names, one meaning 'hero', the other meaning 'hawthorn'.

Haley

Other forms: **Hailey**, **Hayley**

English – place name; from a place in Yorkshire, the name deriving from Old English meaning 'hay' + 'clearing'.

Halifax

English – place name; from the place in Yorkshire, the name deriving from Old English meaning 'field of flax owned by the church'.

Halliday

N English and Scottish – nickname; from Old English meaning 'holy day'.

Halliwell

N English and Scottish – place name; from one of the many places of this name, deriving from Old English meaning 'holy' + 'well, spring'.

Halloway other form of **Alloway**

Hallowes

English – place name; from Old English meaning 'at the nook, enclosure'.

Halton

English – place name; from a place in Cheshire, the name deriving from Old English meaning 'nook, recess' + 'settlement.'

Hamburgh, **Hambury** other forms of **Hanbury**

Hame other form of **Hammond**

Hamilton

Scottish – place name; not from the town in Lanarkshire (which is called after the family) but from a place (or places) in England, the name(s) deriving from Old English meaning 'scarred, bare' + 'hill'. It is the family name of the Dukes of Hamilton.

Hammond

Other forms: **Ha(i)me**

English – personal name; from three possible names:

1 Norman-French **Hamon** of Germanic origin, the first element meaning 'home'.

2 Old Norse **Hámundr** meaning 'high' + 'protection'.

3 Old Norse **Amundr** meaning 'ancestor' + 'protection'.

Hampden

English – place name; from a place in Buckinghamshire, the name deriving from Old English meaning 'water meadow' + 'valley'.

Hampshire

English – place name; either from the county so-named, the name deriving from Hampton + 'division', or from Hallamshire in Yorkshire, the name deriving from **Hallam** + 'division'.

Hanbury

Other forms: **Hamburgh**, **Hambury**

English – place name; from places in Staffordshire and Worcestershire, the name deriving from Old English meaning 'at the high fortress'.

Hancock

English – personal name; from the Middle English name **Hann**, itself probably a form of **John** with the ending '-cock' which came to be attached to certain names to signify 'young'.

Handley other form of **Hanley**

Hankin

English – personal name; from the Middle English name **Hann**, itself probably a form of **John**, + the diminutive '-kin'.

Hanley

Other form: **Handley**

English – place name; from places in Cheshire and Staffordshire, the name deriving from Old English meaning 'high' + 'clearing'.

Hannington

English – place name; from a place in Wiltshire, the name deriving from Old English meaning 'cock' + 'hill'.

Hanrahan

Irish – personal name; anglicized form of Irish Gaelic **Ó Hanrhadháin**, 'descendant of **Anradhán**', itself meaning 'hero'

Hanratty

Irish – personal name/occupational; anglicized form of Irish Gaelic **Ó Hinreachtaigh**, 'descendant of the lawyer'.

Hanry other form of **Henry**

Hansard

English – occupational; from Norman-French of Germanic origin, meaning 'hand' + 'knife', referring to the job of cutler. Luke Hansard (1752–1828) first printed the reports of British parliamentary proceedings which have since been associated with his name.

Hansford

English – place name; possibly from a place in Somerset, the name deriving from an Old English personal name **Ealhmund** meaning 'temple' + 'protection'.

Hanson

English – personal name; from the medieval name **Hann**, itself possibly a form of **John.**

Harbard, Harbart other forms of Herbert

Harbottle

English – place name; from a place in the Cheviots, the name deriving from Old English meaning 'hired man' + 'dwelling'.

Hardcastle

English – place name; from a place in Yorkshire, the name deriving from Middle English meaning 'inaccessible, hard' + 'castle'.

Hardie Scottish form of Hardy

Hardisty

English – place name; from a place in Yorkshire, the name deriving from an Old English personal name meaning 'brave'+ 'wolf' + 'path'.

Hardstaff

English – The name is of uncertain origin, but two possibilities are:
1 nickname; from Middle English meaning 'hard' + 'rod'.
2 place name; from a place in Derbyshire, the name deriving from Old English meaning 'hart' + 'site'.

Hardy

Other form: **Hardie** (Scottish)
English and Scottish – nickname; from Middle English meaning 'bold, brave'.

Harewood other form of Harwood

Hargrave, Hargraves other forms of Hargreave

Hargreave

Other forms: **Hargrave(s)**, **Hargreave(s)**, **Hargreves**, **Hargrove(s)**
English – place name; from many parts of England, the name deriving from Old English meaning 'grey' or 'hare' + 'grove' or 'thicket'.

Harkness

Scottish – place name; from an unidentified place, possibly deriving from an Old English personal name + 'headland'. The name is first recorded in SW Scotland.

Harland

English – place name; from Old English meaning 'grey' or 'hare' + 'piece of land'.

Harley

English – place name; from places in Shropshire and Yorkshire, the name deriving from Old English meaning 'rock' + 'clearing'.

Harlin other form of **Harling**

Harling

Other forms: **Harlin, Hurlen, Hurlin(g)**

English – personal name; from Norman-French of Germanic origin meaning 'warrior' + 'friend'.

Harlock other form of **Horlock**

Harlow

English – place name; from places in Yorkshire and Essex, the name of the former deriving from Old English meaning 'rock' + 'hill'; the places in Essex are probably from Old English meaning 'host' or 'army'.

Harman

Other form: **Harmon**

English – occupational; from Old English meaning 'army' + 'man', referring to a soldier.

Harries other form of **Harris**

Harris

Other forms: **Harries, Harrison**

English – personal name; from **Harry**, a familiar form of **Henry**, itself from Norman-French of Germanic origin meaning 'home ruler'.

Harrismith other form of **Arrowsmith**

Harrison other form of **Harris**

Harrow

English – place name; from the place in London, the name deriving from Old English meaning 'temple', referring to a non-Christian temple.

Harrowsmith other form of **Arrowsmith**

Hartley

English – place name; from many places, the name deriving from Old English meaning 'hart' + 'clearing'.

Hartnell

English – personal name/place name; of uncertain origin, possibly from an Old English name **Heorta**, itself meaning 'hart, stag' + either 'hill' or 'nook, recess'. Alternatively, it may be from Hartnoll in Devonshire. See **Hartnoll**.

Hartnoll

Other form: **Hartnell**

English – place name; from a place near Marwood in Devonshire, the name deriving from Old English meaning 'hart, stag' + 'hill'.

Harvey

Other forms: **Harvie** (Scottish), **Hervey**

English and Scottish – personal name; from a Breton name meaning 'battle' + 'worthy'. The name came to Britain in the wake of the Norman Conquest.

Harwood

Other form: **Harewood**

English and Scottish – place name; from places in the Scottish Borders and in Lancashire and Yorkshire, the name deriving from Old English meaning 'grey' or 'hare' + 'wood'.

Haselden, **Haseldene** other form of **Hazelden**

Haslam

Other forms: **Aslam**, **Aslen**, **Haslan**, **Haslem**

English – place name; from a place in Lancashire, the name deriving from Old English meaning 'hazel'.

Hasletine other form of **Hazelden**

Hassall

Other form: **Hassell**

English – place name; from a place in Cheshire, the name deriving either from an Old English name **Hat** + 'nook or recess' or from Old English meaning 'witch' + 'nook or recess'.

Hatfield

Other forms: **Hatful**, **Hadfield**

English – place name; from many places, the name deriving from Old English meaning 'heath' + 'land'.

Hathaway
Other form: **Hadaway**
English
1 place name; from Old English meaning 'path' + 'way'
2 personal name; from **Hethuig**, an Old English female name deriving from Old English meaning 'strife' + 'war'. Ann Hathaway (b 1556) was the wife of William Shakespeare.

Hattersley
English – place name; from a place in Cheshire, the name deriving from Old English, probably meaning 'deer or stag' + 'clearing'.

Hatton
English – place name; from numerous places throughout England, the name deriving from Old English meaning 'heath' + 'settlement'.

Hattrick other form of **Arkwright**

Haugh other form of **Hale**

Haughey
Irish – personal name; anglicized form of Irish Gaelic **Ó heachadh**, meaning 'descendant of **Eachaidh**'.

Haughton
English – place name; from numerous places in England, the name deriving from Old English meaning 'nook or recess' + 'settlement'.

Haversham, **Havisham** other forms of **Habersham**

Hawken other form of **Hawkins**

Hawkeswood
English – place name; probably from places in Shropshire, the name deriving either from an Old English personal name **Heafoc** + 'wood', or from an Old English name **Hocc** + 'wood'.

Hawking other form of **Hawkins**

Hawkins
Other forms: **Hawking, Hawken**
English – personal name; either from the Middle English name **Hawk** or from a familiar form of **Hal**, itself a familiar form of **Harry** + the diminutive '-kin'.

Hawley
English – place name; from many places, the name deriving usually from Old English meaning 'holy' + 'clearing', referring to a sacred grove. However, in some cases the name derives from Hawley in

Yorkshire from Old Norse meaning 'mound' + Old English meaning 'clearing'.

Haworth
English
1 place name; from the place in West Yorkshire from Old English meaning 'enclosure'.
2 place name; other form of **Howarth.**

Hay
1 Scottish – place name; from various place names in Normandy deriving from French meaning 'hedge'. It is the family name of several Scottish aristocratic families.
2 English – nickname; for a tall person from Middle English meaning 'tall'.

Hayer other form of **Ayer**

Hayes
Other form: **Hey(e)s**
1 English – place name; from various places in Kent, Dorset and Devon, the name deriving either from Old English meaning 'brushwood' or from Middle English meaning 'enclosure'.
2 personal name; anglicized form of Irish Gaelic **Ó Haodha**, itself meaning 'descendant of **Aodh**'

Hayley other form of **Haley**

Hayn, Hayne other forms of **Hain**

Hazelden
Other forms: **Hasleden(e)**, **Hasletine**, **Hazledine**, **Hazletine**, **Heseltine**
English – place name; from Old English meaning 'hazel' + 'valley'.

Headlam
English – place name; from Old English meaning 'at the heathery clearings'.

Headley
English
1 place name; from Old English meaning 'heathery clearing'.
2 place name; other form of **Hadley.**

Heal, Heale, other forms of **Hale**

Heald
English – place name; from a place in Greater Manchester, the name deriving from Old English meaning 'slope'.

Healey
Other form: **Healy**
1 English – place name; from Old English meaning 'high' + 'clearing'.
2 Irish – personal name; anglicized form of Irish Gaelic **Ó hEilidhe**, itself meaning 'descendant of the claimant'.

Heaney
Irish – personal name; anglicized form of Irish Gaelic **Ó hÉanna**, itself meaning 'descendant of **Eanna**'.

Heard
Other forms: **Herd, Hird, Hurd**
English – occupational; from Middle English meaning 'someone who tended animals'.

Hearne other form of **Aherne**

Hebbert other form of **Herbert**

Hedgecock other form of **Hick**

Heffer
Other form: **Hefferman**
English – occupational; from Middle English meaning 'young cow, heifer', referring to a cowherd.

Heggie
Scottish – personal name; shortened from Scottish Gaelic **Mac Adhamh** or **Mac Edhamh**, meaning 'son of **Adam.**'

Hele other form of **Hale**

Henderson
Scottish – personal name; meaning 'son of **Henry**'.

Hendrick other form of **Henry**

Hendry, Hendrie, Henries other forms of **Henry.**

Henries other form of **Henry**

Henry
Other forms: **Hanry, Hendrick, Hendrie, Hendry, Henries, Henryson, Her(r)iot**
English – personal name; from Norman-French of Germanic origin meaning 'home ruler'.

Hepburn
N English and Scottish – place name; from places in Northumberland and Durham, the name deriving from Old English meaning 'high' +

'burial mound' or 'wild rose' + 'stream'. It was the family name of the Earl of Bothwell, third husband of Mary, Queen of Scots.

Herbert
Other forms: **Harbard**, **Harbart**, **Hebbert**, **Herbertson**
English – personal name; from Norman-French of Germanic origin meaning 'army' + 'bright'.

Herd other form of **Heard**

Heriot, **Herriot** other forms of **Henry**

Hervey other form of **Harvey**

Heseltine other form of **Hazelden**

Hew other form of **Hugh**

Hewett other form of **Hewitt**

Hewitt
Other forms: **Hewett**, **Howatt**
English – personal name; from the medieval name **Huet**, itself a form of **Hugh**.

Hewson other form of **Hugh**

Heyer other form of **Ayer**

Heyes, **Heys** other forms of **Hayes**

Hick
Other forms: **Icke**, **Hedgecock**, **Hicken**, **Hickock**, **Hicks**, **Hickson**, **Higgins**, **Higgs**, **Higson**, **Hitch**, **Hitchcock**, **Hitchin**
English – personal name; from the medieval name **Hicke**, itself a familiar form of **Richard**. The latter name came to England by way of Norman French and the initial 'h' represents the English attempt to pronounce a French 'r' sound.

Hiddleston, **Hiddlestone** Scottish forms of **Huddleston**

Hide other form of **Hyde**

Higgins other form of **Hick**

Higgs other form of **Hick**

Highet other form of **Highgate**

Highgate
Other form: **Highet**
Scottish – place name; probably from a place in Ayrshire, the name with obvious meaning.

Higson other form of **Hick**

Hill

Other form: **Hills**

English – place name; from Old English meaning 'hill'. Rowland Hill (1795–1879) was the English originator of the penny post.

Hird other form of **Heard**

Hislop

Other form: **Hyslop**

English – place name; from Old English meaning 'hazel' + 'valley'.

Hitch other form of **Hick**

Hitchcock other form of **Hick**

Hitchin other form of **Hick**

Hobbs

Other forms: **Hobbes, Hobson, Hopkins, Hopson**

English – personal name; from the medieval name **Hobb**, itself a familiar form of **Robert**. Anthony Hopkins (1937–) is a Welsh actor.

Hodge

Other forms: **Hodgkins, Hotchkins, Hotchkiss, Hodgekinson**

English – personal name; from the medieval name **Hodge**, itself a familiar form of **Roger**.

Hogg

Scottish and N English – occupational; from the animal, referring to someone who looked after pigs. In Scotland, however, the word refers to a young sheep. James Hogg, the Ettrick Shepherd (1770–1835), was a Scottish poet and novelist.

Holden

English – place name; from places in Lancashire and Yorkshire, the name deriving from Old English meaning 'hollow' + 'valley'.

Holme

Other forms: **Holmes, Home, Hume.**

Scottish – place name; from the lands of Hume in Berwickshire, the name deriving from northern Middle English probably meaning 'holly tree'. Both Home and Hume are pronounced [hume]. David Hume (1711–76) was a Scottish philospher and historian.

Hope

English and Scottish – place name; from Old English meaning 'valley'.

Hopkins other form of **Hobbs**

Hopson other form of **Hobbs**

Hopwood

English – place name; from a place in Lancashire, the name deriving from Old English meaning 'valley among hills' + 'wood'.

Horlick other form of **Horlock**

Horlock

Other forms: **Harlock, Horlick**

English – nickname; from Old English meaning 'grey' + 'lock of hair', for an old or prematurely old-looking person.

Horsburgh

Scottish – place name; from the place in Peebles-shire, the name deriving from Old English meaning 'horse' + 'brook'.

Hoseason

Scottish – personal name; from Old Norse meaning 'son of **Aassi**', itself a familiar form of **Oswald**. It is a Shetland name.

Hoskin

Other forms: **Hoskins, Hoskyns, Huskinson, Huskisson**

English – personal name; from the Middle English name **Osekin**, itself from Old English meaning 'god' + the ending '-kin'.

Hotchkins other form of **Hodge**

Hotchkiss other form of **Hodge**

Houston

Scottish – place name; from the place in Renfrewshire, the name meaning 'Hugh's settlement'. Houston in Texas is named after Sam Houston (1793–1863), a soldier and statesman of Ulster-Scots descent.

Howard

English – personal name/occupational; of uncertain origin, possibly from Germanic meaning 'heart' + 'brave', or else from Old English meaning 'ewe' + 'herd', referring to a shepherd.

Howarth

Other form: **Haworth**

English – place name; from a place in Lancashire, the name deriving from Old English meaning 'mound' + 'enclosure'.

Howatt other form of **Hewitt**

Howden
Other form: **Hadden**
Scottish – place name; from the place in Roxburghshire, the name deriving from Old English meaning 'hollow' + 'valley'. See also **Haldane.**

Howe
English – place name; from many places, the name deriving from Old Norse meaning 'hillock' or 'burial mound.'

Howel other form of **Howell**

Howell
Other forms: **Howel(s), Howells**
1 Welsh – personal name; from a Welsh name **Hywel**, itself meaning 'eminent'.
2 English – place name; from a place in Lincolnshire, the name deriving from an Old English name **Huna** + 'stream'.

Huddleston other form of **Huddlestone**

Huddlestone
Other forms: **Hiddleston(e), Huddleston**
English, Scottish and N Irish – place name; from places in Yorkshire and Dumfries-shire, the name deriving from an Old English personal name + 'settlement'.

Huggett other form of **Hugh**

Huggins other form of **Hugh**

Hugh
Other forms: **Hughes, Hew, Huggett, Huws, Hewson, Huggins**
English – personal name; from **Hugh**, itself from Norman-French of Germanic origin meaning 'mind, spirit'. See also **Hewitt.**

Hume other form of **Holme**

Humfrey other form of **Humphreys**

Humpherson, Humphrey other forms of **Humphreys**

Humphreys
Other forms: **Humfrey, Humpherson, Humphrey**
English – personal name; from Norman-French of Germanic origin, meaning 'warrior' + 'peace'.

Hunt
Other forms: **Hunte, Hunter**
English – occupational; from Old English meaning 'huntsman'.

Hurd other form of **Heard**

Hurle other form of **Earl**

Hurlen, **Hurlin**, **Hurling** other forms of **Harling**

Huskinson, **Huskisson** other forms of **Hoskin**

Hutchence, **Hutchens**, **Hutchins** other forms of **Hutchinson**

Hutchinson
Other forms: **Hutchence**, **Hutchens**, **Hutchins**
English – personal name; from a diminutive form of **Hugh**. See **Hugh.**

Huws other form of **Hugh**

Huxley
English – place name; from a place in Cheshire, the second part of the name deriving from Old English meaning 'field. open space', the first of uncertain origin, possibly an Old English name. Aldous Huxley (1894–1963) was an English novelist.

Hyde
Other form: **Hide**
English – place name; from Old English meaning one hide of land (varying from 60 to 120 acres), a size calculated to support one extended family.

Hyslop other form of **Hislop**

I

Ibell, **Ibbetson** other form of **Ibbett**

Ibbett
Other forms: **Ibell**, **Ibbetson**, **Ibbotson**
English – personal name; from a familiar form of **Isabel**, a Spanish
form of **Elizabeth**, itself from Hebrew meaning 'God is perfection'.

Icke other form of **Hick**

Idell other form of **Idle**

Idle
Other forms: **Idell**, **Ithell** (Welsh)
English
1 nickname; from Middle English meaning 'lazy'.
2 place name; from a place in Yorkshire, the name deriving from Old
English meaning 'waste ground'.
3 Other form of **Isles**
4 Welsh – personal name; from an Old Welsh personal name **Ithel.**

Iles other form of **Isles**

Illingsworth
Other form: **Illingworth**
English – place name; from a place in Yorkshire, the name deriving
from an Old English personal name **Illa** + 'enclosure'.

Ilsley
English – place name; from a place in Berkshire, the name deriving
from Old English meaning 'battle' + 'clearing'.

Imms
English – personal name; from a Middle English name **Imma**, itself of
Germanic origin meaning 'whole'.

Impey
English – place name; from many small places throughout England,
the name deriving from Old English meaning 'sapling' + 'enclosure'.

Imrie
Scottish – personal name; from Amalric, a Norman-French name of
Germanic origin meaning 'bravery' + 'power'.

Ince

English – place name; from places in Lancashire and Cheshire, the name deriving from Old Welsh meaning 'island'. Compare **Inch.**

Inch

Scottish – place name; from one of the many places of this name (or containing this element), itself from Gaelic meaning 'island' or 'river meadow'. See also **Innes** and compare **Ince.**

Inchbald

English – personal name; from a Germanic personal name, itself meaning 'angel' + 'brave'.

Ingham

English

1 place name; from places in Lincolnshire, Norfolk and Suffolk, the name deriving from the Old English personal name **Inga** + 'homestead'.

2 nickname; for a crafty person from Norman-French meaning 'ingenious, cunning'.

Ingle other form of **Inglis**

Ingleby

English – place name; from places in Yorkshire, Lincolnshire and Derbyshire, the name deriving from Old Norse meaning 'settlement of the English'.

Inglis

Other form: **Ingle**

Scottish – [pronounced 'ingles']

nickname; from Older Scots meaning 'English'.

Ingram

English – personal name; from a Germanic personal name, itself meaning 'angel' + 'raven'.

Inman

English – occupational; from Middle English meaning 'keeper of an inn'.

Innes

Scottish

1 place name; from the lands in Morayshire, the name deriving from Scottish Gaelic meaning 'island' or 'river meadow'. See also **Inch.**

2 personal name; from Scottish Gaelic **Aonghus**, anglicized as **Angus.**

Inskip
English – place name; of uncertain origin, possibly from Old Welsh meaning 'island' + Old English meaning 'fishing basket'.

Ion other form of John

Ireby
English – place name; from places in N Engand, the name deriving from Old Norse meaning 'settlement of the Irish'.

Ireland
English and Scottish – place name; originally denoting someone who came from that country. John Ireland was the name of a 15th-century Scottish philosopher and theologian and of a much later English composer (1879–1962).

Ireton
English – place name; from places in Derbyshire, Yorkshire or Cumbria, the name deriving from one or other of two sources, either from Old English meaning 'Irishmen' + 'settlement' or from the name of the Cumbrian River Irt + 'settlement'.

Irons
English – place name; from a place in Sommes, France, the name deriving from Latin meaning 'sands' and not from the metal.

Ironside
1 English – nickname; from Old English meaning 'iron' + 'side', giving rise to a nickname in Middle English referring to an armoured warrior.
2 Scottish – place name; from a place in Aberdeenshire, the name deriving from a Gaelic river name, or from Old English meaning 'eagle'.

Irvine
Other forms: **Irving, Irwin, Urwin**
Scottish and N Irish – place name; either from Irving, an old Dumfries-shire name or from Irvine in Ayrshire, the name deriving from an old Celtic river name. A NE family of Irvines have lived at Drum Castle in Aberdeenshire since the 14th century.

Isaacs
Other form: **Isa(a)cson**
English – personal name; Biblical, probably from Hebrew meaning 'laugh'.

Isabell

English – personal name; from the Spanish form of Elizabeth, itself Biblical from Hebrew meaning 'God is perfection'. Compare **Ibbett.**

Isacson other form of **Isaacs**

Isard other form of **Izard**

Isherwood

Other forms: **Esherwood, Usherwood**

English – place name; from an unknown place in Lancashire.

Isles

Other forms: **Idle, Iles**

English – place name; from Norman-French meaning 'island'.

Islip

English – place name; from places in Northamptonshire and Oxfordshire, the first deriving from the River Ise, from Old Welsh meaning 'water' + Old English meaning 'slipway', the second from the River Ight + Old English meaning 'slipway'.

Ithell Welsh form of **Idle**

Iverson other form of **Ivor**

Ivey

English – personal name; from a Norman-French name, itself from Old Norse meaning 'yew bow'.

Ivor

Other form: **Iverson**

English – personal name; from Old Norse meaning 'yew bow'.

Izard

Other forms: **Isard, Izzard, Izat(t), Izod, Izzett,**

English – personal name; from **Isolde.** itself from Norman-French of Germanic origin, meaning 'ice' + 'battle'.

J

Jack
Other forms: **Jake, Jakeman, Jagg, Ja(c)ques, Jacklin, Jackson**
Scottish and English – personal name; from one or other of two
sources, from the French first name **Jacques**, a form of **James,** or
from a familiar form of **John.** Glenda Jackson (1936–) is an English
actress and Labour politician.

Jackman
English – occupational; referring to the servant of someone called
Jack.

Jackson other form of **Jack**

Jacob
Other form: **Jacobs, Jacobson, Jacoby**
English – personal name; from Latin **Jacobus,** itself of Hebrew origin
meaning either 'heel' or 'he supplanted', the latter referring to the
Biblical story of Jacob who persuaded his brother Esau to exchange
his birthright, as elder brother, for a mess of pottage. The names **Jacob**
and **James** are from the same origin, but are quite separate names in
English. See also **James.**

Jacques [pronounced **jay-**kweez, jacks or jakes] other form of **Jack**

Jaffry other form of **Jeffrey**

Jagg other form of **Jack**

Jagger
English – occupational; from Middle English meaning 'carter' or
'hawker'. Mick Jagger (1943–) is a member of the Rolling Stones pop
group.

Jago Welsh and Cornish form of **James**

Jake other form of **Jack**

Jakeman other form of **Jack**

James
Other forms: **Jago** (Welsh and Cornish), **Jameson, Jamieson**
English – personal name; from Latin **Jacobus,** itself from Hebrew,

meaning either 'heel' or 'he supplanted', referring to the Biblical story of Jacob who persuaded his brother Esau to exchange his birthright as elder brother for a mess of pottage. The first name **James** has the same origin as **Jacob**, though they are regarded as separate names in English. See also **Jacob.**

Jamieson Scottish form of **Jameson** [usually pronounced **jim-**ison]. See **James.**

Jannings other form of **Jennings**

Jaques other form of **Jack**

Jaram other form of **Jerome**

Jardin other form of **Jardine**

Jardine
Other form: **Jardin**
Scottish
1 place name/occupational; from Old French meaning 'garden', referring to someone who lived in or near one or who worked as a gardener.
2 occupational; other form of **Gardner.**

Jarrard, **Jarratt**, **Jarrett** other forms of **Garrett**

Jarvie Scottish form of **Jarvis.**

Jarvis
English – Other forms: **Gervase**, **Gervis**, **Jarvie** (Scottish), **Jervis** (Scottish)
1 personal name; from the first name **Gervase**, itself from Norman-French of Germanic origin.
2 place name; from Jervaulx in Yorkshire, the name deriving from the name of the River Ure and Norman-French meaning 'valley'.

Jay
Other form: **Jay(e)s**
English – nickname; from the name of the bird, referring to a babbling, showy kind of person.

Jeavon
Other form: **Jeavons**
1 English – nickname; from French meaning 'young'.
2 Welsh – personal name; from the Welsh personal name **Ievan**, itself an earlier form of **Ewan**, a Welsh form of **John.**

Jeeves
Other forms: **Geaves, Geeves**
English – personal name; from **Geva**, a familiar form of **Genevieve**, itself of uncertain origin.

Jeff other form of **Jeffrey**

Jeffrey
Other forms: **Geoffrey, Jaffry, Jeffreys, Jeff(s), Jephcott, Jepp, Jeps, Jepson,**
English – personal name; from Norman-French of Germanic origin, possibly meaning 'sing' or 'territory'. It appears that several names have fused to form the present one, including the first name **Godfrey.**

Jekell other form of **Jekyll**

Jekyll
Other forms: **Jekell, Jewel, Joel, Jowle**
English – personal name; from a Celtic personal name **Iudicael**, itself meaning 'lord' + 'generous'.

Jellett other form of **Gillett**

Jenkins
Other form: **Jenkin, Jinkin(s)**
English – personal name; from the personal name **John** + 'son'.

Jenks
Other form: **Jinks**
English – personal name; from the Middle English personal name **Jenk**, itself from **Jenkin.**

Jennens other form of **Jennings**

Jenner
Other forms: **Genner, Genower, Ginner, Jenoure**
English – occupational; from Middle English meaning 'engineer or designer'.

Jenning
Other forms: **Jannings, Jennens, Jennin(s)**
English – personal name; from the Middle English personal name **Janyn** or **Jenyn**, itself a form of **John.**

Jenoure other form of **Jenner**

Jent, Jentle other forms of **Gentle**

Jephcott other form of **Jeffrey**

Jepp other form of **Jeffrey**

Jeps, Jepson other forms of **Jeffrey**

Jerome
Other forms: **Jaram, Jerram, Jerran, Jerrome**
English – personal name; from a gradual fusion of two personal
names. One name, **Jerome**, came into use in the Middle Ages from a
French name of Greek origin, the other, **Gerram**, is Norman-French
of Germanic origin meaning 'spear' + 'raven'.

Jerrold other form of **Garrett**

Jerrome other form of **Jerome**

Jerrott other form of **Garrett**

Jervis other form of **Jarvis**

Jewel other form of **Jekyll**

Jewry other form of **Jury**

Jillett, Jillitt other forms of **Gillett**

Jinkin, Jinkins other forms of **Jenkins**

Jinks other form of **Jenks**

Joans other form of **Jones**

Joel other form of **Jekyll**

John
Other forms: **Ion, Johns, Johnson, Jon, Jone**
English – personal name; from the first name **John**, itself from
Hebrew, meaning 'God is gracious'. In its various forms, this name
has given rise to many surnames. Samuel Johnson (1709–84) was an
English critic and lexicographer.

Johnston
Other form: **Johnstone**
Scottish – place name; meaning 'John's settlement', referring to one of
the many places of this name in Scotland, in particular to lands in
Annandale in Dumfries-shire, owned by the ancestor of many of the
name.

Joice other form of **Joyce**

Jon, Jone other forms of **John**

Jones
Other forms: **Joans, Joynes**
Welsh and English – personal name; from the medieval first name
Jon(e) which is a form of **John**.

Jordan
Other forms: **Jordin, Jordon, Jourdan**
English – personal name; from a medieval first name, itself from the
name of the River Jordan, the name deriving from Hebrew meaning
'to go down'. Crusaders to the Holy Land often returned home with
bottles of water from the river to baptise their children. Thus the name
had a special significance. See also **Judd.**

Joscelyn
Other forms: **Gosling, Josselyn, Joscelyne, Jos(e)land, Josling**
personal name; from a surname of Norman-French origin probably
based on the name of a Germanic tribe.

Joseland, Josland, Josling other forms of **Joscelyn**

Joseph
English – personal name; from the first name, itself from Hebrew
meaning 'God will add'.

Joss other form of **Joyce**

Josselyn other form of **Joscelyn**

Jourdan other form **Jordan**

Jowle other form of **Jekyll**

Joyce
Other forms: **Joice, Joss**
English and Irish – personal name; from a French form of the Latin
name **Jodocus** which was the name of a 7th-century Breton saint. It
began as a male name, but began to be used as a female name in the
20th century. James Joyce (1882–1941) was an Irish novelist.

Joynes other form of **Jones**

Judd
English – personal name; either from the personal name **Jude**, itself
from Hebrew meaning 'God leads', or else from a familiar form of
Jordan. See **Jordan.**

Jury
Other form: **Jewry**
English – place name; from Middle English meaning 'Jewish quarter',
referring to the area in a medieval town designated for Jews. This
name is likely to refer to a gentile living in the Jewish quarter.

K

Kain, **Kaine**, **Kaines** other forms of **Keynes**

Kaine, **Kayne** other forms of **Cain**

Kavanagh
Other form: **Cavana(u)gh**
Irish – personal name; anglicized form of the Irish Gaelic personal name **Caomhánach**, meaning 'follower of St Caomhán', itself meaning 'tender, gentle'.

Kay
Other forms: **Keay**, **Keye**, **Keyes**, **Atkey**
English
1 occupational; from Old English meaning 'key', referring to a key-maker or someone in public office in charge of ceremonial keys.
2 place name; from Middle English meaning 'quay'.
3 nickname; from Northern Middle English meaning 'jackdaw', referring to a chatterer.
4 nickname; from Danish meaning 'lefthanded'.
5 personal name; from a medieval name of uncertain origin, possibly Old Welsh and based on Latin **Gaius** or **Caius.**

Keagan
Irish
1 personal name; anglicized form of Irish Gaelic **Mac Aodhagáin**, itself meaning 'fire'.
2 personal name; anglicized form of Irish Gaelic **Mac Thadhgáin**, itself probably meaning 'poet'.

Kean other form of **Keane**

Keane
Other forms: Cahane, **Kane**, **Kaynes**, **Kean**
1 English – Other form of **Keen**
2 Irish – personal name; anglicized form of Irish Gaelic **Ó Catháin**, 'descendant of **Cathán**,' itself meaning 'battle'.

Keary other form of **Carey**

Keate, **Keates**, **Keating** other forms of **Kite**

Keay other form of **Kay**

Keel, **Keele** other forms of **Keeler**

Keeler
Other form: **Keel(e)**
English – occupational; from Middle English meaning 'ship', referring to someone who sailed barges or built boats. Compare **Keiller**.

Keen other form of **Keane**

Keep
English – occupational; from Middle English meaning 'keep', referring to a person employed in the dungeon of a castle.

Keery other form of **Carey**

Keet other form of **Kite**

Keiller
Other form: **Keillor**
Scottish – place name; from the place in Angus, probably originally a river name, of the same origin as Calder. The name is well known from the Dundee marmalade manufacturer. Compare **Keeler**.

Keir
Scottish
1 place name; probably from the place in Stirlingshire, the name deriving from Old Welsh meaning 'fort'.
2 nickname; from Scottish Gaelic meaning 'dark, swarthy'.

Keith
Scottish – place name; from the lands in East Lothian, the name deriving from Old Welsh meaning 'wood'. The Keith family were hereditary Earls Marischal in Scotland from the 15th to the 18th century.

Kell other form of **Kettle**

Kellogg
English – occupational; from Middle English meaning 'to kill' + 'hog', referring to the occupation of pork butcher or slaughterer. John and Will Kellogg were 19th-century American inventors who processed wheat and corn to make a breakfast cereal.

Kelly
1 Irish – personal name; anglicized form of Irish Gaelic **Ó Ceallaigh**, itself from Irish Gaelic meaning 'troublesome'.
2 Scottish – place name; from various places of this name, especially

one near Arbroath in Angus. The name probably derives from Scottish Gaelic meaning 'wood'.

Kelman

Scottish – place name; from Kelman Hill in Aberdeenshire, itself probably deriving from Scottish Gaelic meaning 'narrow hill'. James Kelman (1946–) is a Glasgow novelist.

Kelso

Scottish – place name; from the town in Roxburghshire, the name probably deriving from Old English meaning 'chalk' + 'precipice, crag'.

Kemble

1 English – personal name; from the medieval name **Kimbel**, itself from Old English meaning 'royal' + 'brave'.

2 English – place name; from a place in Gloucestershire, the name deriving from Old Welsh meaning 'border'.

3 Welsh – personal name; from a Celtic name meaning 'chief' + 'war'.

Kemp

English – occupational; from Middle English meaning 'warrior, champion', referring to a champion wrestler or jouster.

Kendall

Other forms: **Kendell**, **Kendle**, **Kindal(l)**

English – place name; from places in Yorkshire and Cumbria, the name of the former deriving from Old English meaning 'spring' + 'valley', the name of the latter from the River Kent + 'valley'.

Kendrick other form of Kenrick

Kenneally

Other form: **Kennelly**

Irish – personal name; anglicized form of Irish Gaelic **Ó Cionnfhaolaidh**, descendant of **Cionnfhaoladh**, itself meaning 'head' + 'wolf'.

Kennedy

Irish and Scottish – personal name; anglicized form of Gaelic **Ó Cinnéidigh**, descendant of **Cinnéidigh**, probably meaning 'ugly-headed'. The Irish Kennedys claim descent from Brian Boru, the 11th-century King of Ireland, The Scottish family originated in SW Scotland. John F Kennedy (1917–63) was 35th president of the United States.

Kennett

English – place name; from a place in Wiltshire, the name deriving from the River Kennet on which it stands.

Kenrick

Other form: **Kendrick**

English – personal name; from an Old Welsh personal name **Cynwryg** meaning 'chief' + 'hero'.

Kenyon

English – place name; from a place in Lancashire, the name probably deriving from Old Welsh 'mound' + a personal name.

Ker other form of **Kerr**

Kermode

Other form: **Carmode**

Manx – personal name; Manx form of the personal name **Dermott.**

Kerr

Other forms: **Ker, Carr**

Scottish and N English – place name; from an Old Norse place-name element, meaning 'rough ground with brushwood'. The theory that it derives from Gaelic meaning 'left-handed' probably comes from a traditional belief that all Kerrs were left-handed.

Kershaw

Other form: **Kirshaw**

English – place name; from a place in Lancashire, the name deriving from Middle English meaning 'church' + 'grove'.

Kettle

Other forms: **Kittle, Kell**

English – personal name; from an Old Norse personal name **Ketill**, itself from Old Norse meaning 'cauldron'.

Keye, **Keyes** other forms of **Kay**

Keynes

Other forms: **Kaines, Caines**

English – place name; from a place in Normandy, the name deriving from a Celtic word meaning 'juniper'.

Keyte other form of **Kite**

Kilbey

Other form: **Kilby**

English – place name; from a place in Leicestershire, the name deriving from Old English meaning 'child' + 'settlement'.

Kilbey other form of **Kilby**

Kilbride

1 Irish – personal name; anglicized form of Irish Gaelic **Mac Giolla Brighde**, itself meaning 'son of the servant of St Bridget'.

2 Scottish – place name; from one of the many places of this name in Scotland, probably East Kilbride in Lanarkshire or West Kilbride in Ayrshire. The name derives from Gaelic meaning 'church of St Bridget'.

Kilgour

Scottish – place name; from the place in Fife, the name deriving from Scottish Gaelic meaning 'wood' + 'goat'.

Kilner

English – occupational; from Old English meaning 'kiln', referring to a potter or lime burner.

Kilpatrick

1 Irish – personal name; anglicized form of Irish Gaelic **Mac Giolla Phádraig**, itself from Irish Gaelic meaning 'son of **Patrick**',

2 Scottish – place name; from places of this name, probably from those in Dumfries-shire and Dunbartonshire. The name derives from Gaelic meaning 'church of St Patrick'.

Kilroy other form of **Gilroy**

Kincey other form of **Kinsey**

Kindal, **Kindall** other forms of **Kendall**

King

English – nickname/occupational; from Old English meaning 'king', referring to someone with a majestic or arrogant manner, or to someone who played the part of a king in a pageant. Martin Luther King (1929–1968) was an American civil rights leader.

Kinghorn

Scottish – place name; from the town in Fife, the name probably deriving from Scottish Gaelic meaning 'head, end' + 'bog'.

Kinloch

Scottish – place name; from one of the many places in Scotland of this name, from Scottish Gaelic meaning 'head, end' + 'lake'. The earliest recording of the surname comes from Kinloch at the head of Rossie Loch in Fife. See also **Lochhead.**

Kinnaird

Scottish – place name; from the lands in Perthshire, the name deriving from Scottish Gaelic meaning 'head, end' + 'height'.

Kinniburgh

Scottish – place name; from Conisborough in Yorkshire, the name deriving from Old English meaning 'rabbit' + 'fort, town'. The surname has been recorded in Scotland, in many different spellings, since the 12th century.

Kinross

Scottish – place name; from the lands in the county of that name, deriving from Scottish Gaelic meaning 'head, end' + 'promontory'.

Kinsey

Other forms: **Kincey**, **Kynsey**

English – personal name; from an Old English personal name meaning 'royal' + 'victory'. Alfred Charles Kinsey (1894–1956) was a sexologist and zoologist, author of the *Kinsey Report*.

Kipling

English – place name; from places in Yorkshire, the name deriving from an Old English personal name **Cyppel** or **Cybbel** of uncertain origin. Rudyard Kipling (1865–1936) was an English writer.

Kirby

Other form: **Kirkby**

English – place name; from places in the north of England, the name deriving from Old English and Old Norse meaning 'church' + 'settlement'.

Kirk

Scottish and N English – place name/occupational; from Old English and Old Norse meaning 'church', referring either to someone who lived near a church, or to someone who worked in one.

Kirkbride

Other form: **Kirkbright**

English – place name; from various places, the name deriving from Old English and Old Norse meaning 'church dedicated to St Bridget'.

Kirkby other form of **Kirby**

Kirkpatrick

Scottish and N Irish – place name; from several places in Dumfries-shire, the name deriving from Old English and old Norse meaning 'church of St Patrick'.

Kirkup

English – place name; from places in Peeblesshire, Selkirkshire and Northumberland, the name deriving from Old English and Old Norse meaning 'church' + 'valley'.

Kirkwood

Scottish – place name; from several places, the name deriving from Old English and Old Norse meaning 'church' + 'wood'.

Kirshaw other form of Kershaw

Kite

Other forms: **Keet**, **Keate(s)**, **Kyte**, **Keyte**, **Keating**

English – nickname; from Middle English meaning 'kite', referring to someone who looked like a bird of prey. John Keats (1795–1821) was an English poet.

Kittle other form of Kettle

Knapman other form of Knapp

Knapp

English – Other forms: **Knapper**, **Knapman**, **Knappman**

place name; from places in Devon and Sussex, the name deriving from Old English meaning 'hilltop'.

Knapton

English – place name; from places in Yorkshire and the Midlands, the name deriving from Old English meaning 'servant' + 'settlement'.

Knatchbull

English – occupational; from Middle English meaning 'to knock on the head' + 'bull', referring to the occupation of slaughterer or butcher.

Knight

English – occupational; from Old English meaning 'youth, servant, medieval tenant bound to serve as a soldier'.

Knockton other form of Naughton

Knoll

Other forms: **Knowles**, **Knollys**

English

1 place name; from places throughout England, the name deriving from Old English meaning 'hilltop'.

2 nickname; from Old English meaning 'hilltop', referring to a squat, lumpish person.

Knott

English

1 nickname; from Old English meaning 'knot, lump', referring to a squat, lumpish person.

2 place name; from a hilly place, the name deriving from Middle English meaning 'a bump or hillock or spur of rock'.

3 personal name; from an Old Norse personal name **Knútr**, probably meaning 'knot or lump'.

Knox

Scottish, N English, N Irish – place name; from Old English meaning 'hill, hillock' with plural or possessive '-s' ending. Many of the name are descended from a family from Knock in Renfrewshire. The most famous bearer was John Knox, the 16th-century Scottish religious reformer.

Kyle

Scottish and N Irish – place name; from the district in Ayrshire, said to derive its name from a 5th-century line of British chieftains. The surname may also derive from other places in Scotland of this name, deriving from Scottish Gaelic meaning 'narrow'.

Kynaston

Scottish – place name; from the lands in Fife, the name deriving from Scottish Gaelic meaning 'head(land)' + 'west'.

Kynsey other form of **Kinsey**

Kyte other form of **Kite**

L

Lacey
Other forms: **Lacy, De Lac(e)y, Lassey**
English and Irish – place name; from a place in Calvados in
Normandy, the name deriving from a Gaulish name **Lascius** of
unknown meaning.

Lacock
English – place name; from a place in Wiltshire, the name deriving
from Old English meaning 'streamlet'. See also **Laycock.**

Lacy other form of **Lacey**

Ladbroke other form of **Ladbrooke**

Ladbrooke
Other form: **Ladbroke**
English – place name; from a place in Warwickshire, the second part
of the name deriving from Old English meaning 'brook', the first part
possibly from Old English meaning 'choice, decision', referring to a
water course used for divining the future.

Ladd
English – occupational; from Middle English meaning 'servant' or
'man of humble birth'.

Lafferty other form of **Laverty**

Laing
Scottish [pronounced **lay-**ing]
nickname; an Older Scots form of 'lang' meaning 'long, tall'. R D
Laing (1927–89) was a controversial Scottish psychiatrist.

Laird
Scottish and N Irish – occupational; from Scots meaning 'landowner'.

Laker
English
1 place name; from a place near a stream, the name deriving from Old
English meaning 'stream'.
2 occupational; from Middle English meaning 'actor'.

Lakin
English – personal name; from a familiar form of **Lawrence.**

Lally other form of **Mullally**

Lamb
Other forms: **Lambie, Lamkin, Lammie, Lampkin, Lampson, Lamson**
English
1 nickname; from Middle English meaning 'lamb', referring to a gentle, docile person.
2 occupational; from Middle English meaning 'lamb', referring to a shepherd.
3 personal name; from a short form of **Lambert.**
4 Irish – personal name; anglicized form of Irish Gaelic **Ó Luain**, descendant of **Luan**, itself meaning 'warrior'. Charles Lamb (1775–1834) was an English essayist.

Lambard other form of **Lambert**

Lambert
Other forms: **Lambard, Lamberton, Lambrick, Lampert**
English – personal name; from Norman-French of Germanic origin, meaning 'land' + 'bright'.

Lambie other form of **Lamb**

Lambourne
English – place name; from places in Essex and Berkshire, the name deriving from Old English meaning 'lamb' + 'stream'.

Lambrick other form of **Lambert**

Lambton
English – place name; from a place in Durham, the name deriving from Old English meaning 'lamb' + 'settlement'.

Lamkin other form of **Lamb**

Lammie other form of **Lamb**

Lamond other form of **Lamont**

Lamont
Other forms: **Lamond**
Scottish and N Irish [usually **la**-mont, **la**-mond]
occupational; from Old Norse meaning 'law man, lawyer'. The family originated in Argyllshire. Frederic Lamond (1868–1948) was a well-known pianist and composer.

Lampert other form of **Lambert**

Lampet
Other forms: **Lampitt**, **Lamputt**
English – place name/occupational; from Middle English meaning 'clay or loam pit', referring to a place where such building materials were excavated, or to a worker in a clay pit.

Lampkin other form of **Lamb**

Lamplough other form of **Lamplugh**

Lamplugh
Other form: **Lamplough**
English – place name; from a place in Cumberland, the name deriving from Old Welsh and Latin, meaning 'parish church' + 'place'.

Lampson other form of **Lamb**

Lamputt other form of **Lampet**

Lamson other form of **Lamb**

Lander other form of **Lavender**

Landseer
English – place name; from Old English meaning 'land' + 'boundary'. Sir Edwin Landseer (1802–73) was an English animal painter.

Lang
Scottish – nickname; from Old English meaning 'long, tall'.

Langdon
Other form: **Longdon**
English – place name; from many places, the name deriving from Old English meaning 'long' + 'hill'.

Langland
Other form: **Langlands**
Scottish and N English – place name; from lands in Peebleshire, the name deriving from Older Scots meaning 'long' + 'land'.

Langley
Other form: **Longley**
English
1 place name; from many places, the name deriving from Old English meaning 'long' + 'clearing'.
2 personal name; from an Old Norse name **Langlif**, meaning 'long life'.

Langmuir
Other forms: **Longmore**, **Longmuir**
Scottish – place name; from various places, the names deriving from Older Scots meaning 'long' + 'moor'.

Langridge
Other form: **Longridge**
English – place name; from many places, the name deriving from Old English meaning 'long' + 'ridge'.

Langtree
Other form: **Langtry**
English – place name; from places in Devonshire, Lancashire and Oxfordshire, the name deriving from Old English meaning 'long' + 'tree'. Lilly Langtry (1853–1929) was a British actress.

Lanyon
Cornish – place name; from the place in Cornwall near Penzance, the name deriving from Cornish meaning 'pool' + 'cold'.

Lappin
Other form: **Lapping**
English – occupational; from French meaning 'rabbit', referring to a dealer or a breeder of rabbits.

Larcombe
English – place name; from places in Devon, the name deriving from Old English, meaning either 'wild iris' or 'lark' + 'valley'.

Larimer other form of **Lorimer**

Lark
Other forms: **Larkman**, **Laverack**, **Laverick**
English
1 nickname/occupational; from Middle English meaning 'lark', referring to a cheerful person, or an early riser, or possibly to someone who made a living by catching and selling birds.
2 personal name; from a medieval name formed from **Lawrence**. See also **Lawrence**.

Larkin
English – personal name; from a medieval name, itself a form of **Lawrence**. See also **Lawrence**.

Larkman other form of **Lark**

Larner
Other form: **Lerner**
English – occupational; from Middle English meaning 'to learn' or 'to teach', referring to either a teacher or a scholar.

Lascelles
English – place name; from a place in France, the name deriving from French meaning 'hermit's cell'.

Lasenby other form of **Lazenby**

Lashford other form of **Latchford**

Lassey other form of **Lacey**

Latcham
English – place name; from a place in Somerset, the name deriving from Old English meaning 'stream' + 'settlement'.

Latchford
Other forms: **Lashford**, **Letchford**
English – place name; from many places, the name deriving from Old English meaning 'stream' + 'ford'.

Latham
Other forms: **Lathem**, **Lathom**
English – place name; from several places in the north of England, the name deriving from Old English meaning 'barn'.

Latimer
Other forms: **Latimore**, **Latner**
English – occupational; from Norman-French meaning 'Latin translator or interpreter'.

Lauder
Scottish and N English – place name; from the town in Berwickshire, the name of obscure origin. Sir Harry Lauder (1870–1950) was a famous Scottish comedian and singer.

Laughton
English – place name; from many places in England, the name deriving from Old English meaning 'leek' + 'enclosure', referring to kitchen or herb gardens in general, rather than just leek beds.

Launder other form of **Lavender**

Laurence other form of **Lawrence**

Laurie other form of **Lawrence**

Lavender
Other forms: **Launder**, **Lander**
English – occupational; from Norman-French meaning 'launderer', referring to a person who washed raw wool before it was processed, or cleaned the finished cloth. See also **Laver.**

Laver
English – occupational; from Norman-French 'to wash', referring to a person who washed raw wool before it was processed, or cleaned the finished cloth. See also **Lavender.**

Laverack, **Laverick** other forms of **Lark**

Laverty
Other form: **Lafferty**
Irish – personal name; anglicized form of Irish Gaelic **Ó Fhlaithbheartaigh**, descendant of **Fhlaithbeartaigh**, itself meaning 'ruler' + 'doer of valiant feats'.

Law
Other form: **Lawson**
English and Scottish
1 personal name; from a medieval familiar form of **Lawrence**.
2 place name; from Northern Middle English meaning 'burial ground, hill'.

Lawley
English – place name; from a place in Shropshire, the name deriving from an Old English personal name meaning 'survivor' + 'clearing'.

Lawrance other form of **Lawrence**

Lawrence
Other forms: **Laurence**, **Laurie**, **Lawrance**, **Lawrenson**, **Lowrie**
English – personal name; from Norman-French of Latin origin, meaning 'man from Laurentum' (a town near Rome). D H Lawrence (1885–1930) was an English writer. See also **Lark**, **Larkin** and **Law.**

Lawson other form of **Law**

Laycock
Other form: **Leacock**
English – place name; from a place in Yorkshire, the name deriving from a diminutive of Old English meaning 'stream'. See also **Lacock.**

Laye, **Lay** other forms of **Lee**

Layland other form of **Leyland**

Lazenby
Other form: **Lasenby**
English – place name; from the place in Yorkshire, the name deriving from Old Norse meaning 'freedman' + 'settlement'.

Lea other form of **Lee**

Leach
Other form: **Leech**
English
1 occupational; from Old English meaning 'leech', referring to a physician.
2 place name; from Old English meaning 'stream'.

Leacock other form of **Laycock**

Leadbetter
English – occupational; from Middle English meaning 'leadbeater', referring to someone who worked in lead.

Leahy
Irish – personal name; anglicized form of Irish Gaelic **Ó Laochdha**, 'descendant of **Laochdh**', itself meaning 'hero'.

Lear
English – place name; either from places in France, the name deriving from Germanic meaning 'clearing', or from a place in Leicestershire, the name deriving from an Old Welsh river name.

Learmond, **Learmont** other forms of **Learmonth**

Learmonth
Other forms: **Learmond**, **Learmont**
Scottish – place name; from the lands in Berwickshire, the name of obscure origin. The Russian poet Mikhail Lermontov (1814–41) was descended from a Scot named Learmont.

Lease
English – place name; from Old English meaning 'pasture'.

Leatherbarrow
English – place name; from a place in Furness, the name deriving from Old Norse meaning 'lair of a wild animal' + Old English meaning 'grove, wood'.

Leaver other form of **Lever**

Leckie

Other form: **Lecky**

Scottish – place name; from the lands in Stirlingshire, the name
deriving from Scottish Gaelic meaning 'having flat stones'.

Lee

Other forms: **Attlee, Lay(e), Lea, Lees, Leigh, Ley, Lye**

1 English – place name; from many places, the name deriving from
Old English meaning 'clearing'.

2 Irish – personal name; anglicized form of Irish Gaelic **Ó Laoidhigh**,
'descendant of **Laoidheach**', itself meaning 'poet'.

Leech other form of **Leach**

Leeming

English

1 place name; from places in Yorkshire, the name deriving from a
river name from Old English meaning 'glitter, sparkle'.

2 nickname/personal name; other form of **Lemon.**

Lees other form of **Lee**

Legatt other form of **Leggatt**

Leggatt

Other forms: **Legatt, Legget(t)**

English – occupational; from Middle English meaning 'appointed,
ordained', referring to the post of legate or ambassador, or to someone
who dressed as a diplomat in pageants.

Leigh other form of **Lee**

Leith

Scottish – place name; from the town, port of Edinburgh, which takes
its name from the river, the Water of Leith. The name probably derives
from Old Welsh meaning 'damp, wet'. A branch of the family moved
in the Middle Ages to Aberdeenshire where the name is still common

Lemon

English

1 personal name; from a Middle English name **Lefman**, itself from
Old English meaning 'beloved' + 'man'.

2 nickname; from Middle English meaning 'sweetheart'. See also
Leeming.

Lennard other form of **Leonard**

Lennie

Scottish – place name; from lands near Callander in Perthshire, the name deriving from the River Leny, itself of obscure (Celtic) origin. The Lennies in Orkney probably derive their name from a local place name.

Lennon

Irish – personal name; anglicized form of Irish Gaelic, either from Ó Leannáin, descendant of Lonán, meaning 'lover', or from Ó Lonáin, descendant of Leannán, itself meaning 'blackbird'. John Winston Lennon (1940–80) was a member of the Beatles pop group.

Lennox

Scottish and N Irish – place name; from the ancient district around Dumbarton, the name probably deriving from Gaelic meaning 'elm-tree'.

Leonard

Other form: **Lennard**

English – personal name; from Norman-French of Germanic origin, meaning 'lion' + 'brave'.

Lerner other form of **Larner**

Leslie

Scottish – place name; from places in Aberdeenshire and Fife (the second probably deriving from the first). The origin of the name is obscure. It is the family name of the Earls of Rothes.

Lester, **Lestor** other forms of **Lister**

Letchford other form of **Latchford**

Lett

Other form: **Letts**

English – personal name; from a familiar form of the female name **Lettice**, itself from Latin meaning 'happiness'.

Lever

Other forms: **Leaver**, **Leverett**

English

1 nickname; from Old French meaning 'hare', referring to a fast runner, or perhaps a timid person.

2 place name; from places in Lancashire, the name deriving from Old English meaning 'reed, rush'.

3 personal name; from an Old English name **Leofhere**, itself meaning 'beloved' + 'army'.

Lewellin other form of **Llewelyn**

Lewin

English – personal name; from a medieval name **Lefwine**, itself from Old English meaning 'dear' + 'friend'.

Lewis

English and Welsh

1 personal name; from **Lowis**, a Norman-French name of Germanic origin, meaning 'fame' + 'war'.

2 personal name; anglicized form of Welsh **Llewelyn.**

Ley other form of **Lee**

Leyland

Other form: **Layland**

English – place name; from a place in Lancashire, the name deriving from Middle English meaning 'land left uncultivated'.

Libby

English – personal name; from a medieval familiar form of **Elizabeth**.

Liddel other form of **Liddell**

Liddell

Other forms: Liddel, Liddle

Scottish [usually pronounced **lid**dle]

place name; from several places of this name in S Scotland and N England, deriving from Old English meaning 'loud' + 'valley'.

Liddiard

English – place name; from Lydiard in Wiltshire, the latter part of the name deriving from Old Welsh meaning 'garth, courtyard'.

Liddiatt

Other forms: **Lidgate**

English – place name; from places in Suffolk or Lancashire, the name deriving from Middle English meaning 'gate between a meadow and a ploughed field.'

Liddle other form of **Liddell**

Lidgate other form of **Liddiatt**

Lilley

English

1 personal name; from a short form of **Elizabeth.**

2 nickname; from Middle English meaning 'lily', referring to someone with fair skin or hair.

3 place name; from places in Hertfordshire and Berkshire, the name deriving, in the first case, from Old English meaning 'flax' + 'clearing'. The second is from an Old English name **Lilla** + 'wood, clearing'.

Lillicrap other form of **Lillicrop**

Lillicrop
Other form: **Lillicrap**
English – nickname; from Old English meaning 'lily' + 'head', referring to someone with fair hair.

Linacre
Other forms: **Linaker**, **Lineker**, **Liniker**
English – place name; from places in Lancashire and Cambridgeshire, the name deriving from Old English meaning 'flax' + 'field'.

Linch other form of **Lynch**

Lindley other form of **Linley**

Lindop
English – place name; from Old English meaning 'lime' + 'valley'.

Lindsay
Other form: **Lindsey**
English and Scottish – place name; probably deriving from Old English meaning 'isle of Lincoln'.

Lineker, **Liniker** other forms of **Linacre**

Linklater
Scottish – place name; from one of the places of this name in the Orkney Islands, deriving from Old Norse meaning 'heather' + 'rock'. Eric Linklater (1899–1974) was a well-known Scottish novelist.

Linley
Other form: **Lindley**
English – place name; from either of two sources, the name in Yorkshire, Wiltshire and Shropshire deriving from Old English meaning 'flax' + 'clearing' and the name of the place near Otley deriving from Old English meaning 'lime tree' + 'clearing'.

Liptrot
English – nickname; of uncertain origin. It has been suggested that it derives from Germanic meaning 'dear' + 'beloved'.

Lisle
Other form: **Lyle**
English – place name; from Middle English meaning 'island', or specifically referring to the French town of Lille, itself meaning 'the island'.

Lister
Other forms: **Lester**, **Lestor**
English – occupational; from Middle English meaning 'dyer'.

Lithgow
Scottish – place name; from the town of Linlithgow in West Lothian, the name probably deriving from Old Welsh meaning 'pool' + 'damp' + 'hollow'.

Litton other form of **Lytton**

Livermore
English – place name; probably from a place in Suffolk, the name deriving from Old English meaning 'reed' + 'mere'.

Livesey
Other forms: **Livesley**, **Livsey**
English – place name; from a place in Lancashire, the name deriving from Old English meaning 'protection' + 'island'.

Livingston other form of **Livingstone**

Livingstone
Other form: **Livingston**
Scottish – place name; from the place near Edinburgh, the name deriving from an Old English personal name, **Leving** + 'settlement'. Some Scottish bearers however descend from a small clan, the MacLeays of Appin, who used Livingstone as an anglicization of their name. To those belonged the missionary and explorer David Livingstone (1813–73).

Livsey other form of **Livesey**

Llewelyn
Other form: **Lewellin**
Welsh – personal name; from Old Welsh probably meaning 'leader'.

Lloyd
Other forms: **Loyd**, **Floyd**
Welsh – nickname; from Welsh meaning 'grey', referring to someone who had grey hair or dressed in grey.

Lochhead
Scottish – place name; denoting someone who lived at the head of a lake. See also **Kinloch.**

Lochrie
Scottish [pronounced **loch**-ree]
place name; probably from Lochrie in Ayrshire or from Lochree in Wigtownshire.

Lock other form of **Lucas**

Lockhart
Scottish [pronounced **lok**-art] personal name; possibly from an Old French name **Locard**, of Germanic origin meaning 'bolt' + 'hard.' There have been Lockharts in central Scotland since the 12th century. J G Lockhart (1794–1854) was the son-in-law and biographer of Sir Walter Scott.

Lodge
English – occupational; from Middle English meaning 'temporary dwelling', probably referring to a mason who used such a cabin during the construction of cathedrals and other great works.

Lofthouse other form of **Loftus**

Loftus
Other form: **Lofthouse**
English – place name; from places in Yorkshire, the name deriving from Old Norse meaning 'loft' + 'house', referring to a dwelling with an upper storey to hold winter fodder and provisions.

Logan
Scottish and N Irish – place name; from one of several places of this name in Scotland, most probably that in Ayrshire. The name derives from Scottish Gaelic meaning 'little hollow'. Jimmy Logan (1928–) is a well-known Scottish comedian.

Logie
Scottish – place name; from one of several places of this name in Scotland, the name deriving from Scottish Gaelic meaning 'full of hollows'.

Lomas other form of **Lomax**

Lomax
Other form: **Lomas**
English – place name; from a place in Lancashire, the name deriving from Old English meaning 'pool' + 'nook, recess'.

Longbotham other form of **Longbottom**

Longbottom
Other form: **Longbotham**
English – place name; probably from the place in West Yorkshire, the name deriving from Middle English meaning 'long valley'.

Longdon other form of **Langdon**

Longley other form of **Langley**

Longmore, **Longmuir** other forms of **Langmuir**

Longridge other form of **Langridge**

Lonsdale
English – place name; from places in Lancashire and Cumbria, the name deriving from Old English meaning 'the valley of the River Lune'.

Lord
English – nickname; from Old English meaning 'loaf keeper', that is, 'lord or chief who provided for his people'. While this could be the name of a ruling family, it is more likely to have been held by someone belonging to a lord's family as a servant. It may also have referred to someone who took the role of a lord in pageants.

Lorimer
Other forms: **Larimer**
English and Scottish – occupational; from Norman-French meaning 'tackle or harness', referrring to a maker of metal parts for tackle and harness.

Lothian
Scottish – place name; from the area in SE Scotland, an ancient name of obscure origin. See also **Loudon.**

Louden other form of **Loudon**

Loudon
Other forms: **Louden**, **Lowden**
Scottish – place name;
1 from Loudon in Ayrshire, the name deriving from an old Celtic personal name + 'fort'.
2 probably another form of **Lothian**.

Lovat
Other forms: Lovatt, **Lovett**, **Lovitt**
English – nickname; from Norman-French of Germanic origin, meaning 'wolf cub'.

Loveday

English

1 personal name; from a Middle English name meaning 'love' + 'day',
2 nickname; from the medieval occasion called 'love day' when
enemies made peace, referring to someone associated with such an
occasion.

Lovelace

English – nickname; from Middle English meaning 'without love',
referring to a breaker of hearts, a philanderer.

Lovell

Other form: **Lowell**

English – nickname; from Norman-French of Germanic origin
meaning 'wolf cub'.

Lovett, Lovitt other forms of **Lovatt**

Low

Other form: **Lowe**

English

1 place name; from places near or on hills, the name deriving from Old
English meaning 'hill' or 'burial mound'.
2 nickname; from Middle English meaning 'short' referring to a small
man.
3 personal name; from a familiar form of **Lawrence**

Lowden other form of **Loudon**

Lowe other form of **Low**

Lowell other form of **Lovell**

Lowrie other form of **Lawrence**

Lowther

English – place name; from a place in Cumbria, the origin of the name
is uncertain, possibly deriving from Old Norse meaning 'froth' +
'river'.

Loyd other form of **Lloyd**

Lucas

Other forms: **Luke**, **Lock**, **Lugg**

English – personal name; from Greek meaning 'man from Lucania',
popular in the Middle Ages because of St Luke the evangelist.

Lumley

English – place name; from a place in County Durham, the name
deriving from Old English meaning 'pool' + 'clearing'.

Lumsden
Scottish – place name; from a place in Berwickshire, the name deriving from a personal name + Old English meaning 'valley'.

Luttrell
English – nickname/occupational; from Old French meaning 'otter', referring to someone who resembled an otter; possibly also referring to a hunter of otters

Lyall
Other form: **Lyell**
English – personal name; probably from an Old Norse personal name, containing the word for 'wolf'.

Lye other form of **Lee**

Lyell other form of **Lyall**

Lyle other form of **Lisle**

Lynch
Other form: **Linch**
1 English – place name; from a places in Somerset and Sussex, the name deriving from Old English meaning 'slope, hillside'.
2 Irish – personal name; anglicized form of Irish Gaelic, either from **Ó Loingsigh**, descendant of **Loingseach**, meaning 'mariner', or from **Linseach**, itself of uncertain origin.

Lyon
Other form: **Lyons**
English
1 nickname; from Middle English meaning 'lion', referring to someone fierce and brave.
2 personal name; from **Leon**, itself from Latin meaning 'lion'.

Lyttelton
Scottish – place name; of unknown origin, although there is a theory that it derives from Ludlow in Shropshire. The name originates from the Borders.

Lytton
Other form: **Litton**
English – place name; from many places including some in Derbyshire and Somerset, the name deriving from Old English meaning 'torrent' + 'settlement'.

M

Mabon
Scottish – personal name; probably from an Old Welsh name meaning 'son'+ 'great'.

Macaleer other form of **McClure**

MacAlister other form of **MacAllister**

Macallan
Scottish – personal name; from Scottish Gaelic meaning 'son of **Alan**'. The name is best known from a brand of Scotch malt whisky.

MacAllister
Other form: **MacAlister**
Scottish – personal name; from Scottish Gaelic meaning 'son of **Alexander**'.

MacAlpin
Other form: **MacAlpine**
Scottish – personal name; from Gaelic meaning 'son of **Alpin**', an old Celtic name of doubtful origin. Kenneth mac Alpin became king of the Scots and later also of the Picts in the 9th century.

MacArthur
Scottish – personal name; from Scottish Gaelic meaning 'son of **Arthur**'. The MacArthurs were a powerful clan in Argyll in the Middle Ages. A famous modern bearer was the American General Douglas MacArthur (1880–1964).

McArtney other form of **McCartney**

MacAskill other form of **MacCaskill.**

MacAulay
Other form: **MacCauley**
Scottish – personal name; from Scottish Gaelic meaning 'son' + a personal name: either from an Old Gaelic personal name, or else from the Old Norse name **Olafr.** Zachary Macaulay (1768–1838) was a philanthropist and slave-trade abolitionist, and father of the historian Lord Macaulay (1800–59).

MacBain

Scottish – nickname; from Scottish Gaelic meaning 'son' + 'fair one'.

MacBeath other form of **Macbeth.**

Macbeth

Other form: **MacBeath**

Scottish – personal name; from a Scottish Gaelic first name meaning literally 'son of life' (probably designating a man of religion). The Macbeth of Shakespeare's play was King of Scots from 1040 (when he murdered Duncan) until 1057. See also **Beaton**.

MacBrayne

Scottish – occupational; from Scottish Gaelic meaning 'son of the judge'. It was the name of a family whose contracting firm controlled much of the transport on the west coast of Scotland in the early and mid 20th century (now subsumed in CalMac). See **Brain.**

MacCallum

Scottish – personal name; from Scottish Gaelic meaning 'son of **Malcolm**'

McCartney

Other form: **McArtney**

Irish and Scottish – personal name; from an old Gaelic name, a familiar form of **Art**, itself meaning 'bear' or 'champion'. Paul McCartney (1942–) is a pop singer and an original member of the Beatles pop group,

MacCaskill

Other form: **MacAskill**

Scottish – personal name; from Scottish Gaelic meaning 'son' + an Old Norse personal name meaning 'gods' + 'kettle' (probably referring to a sacrificial vessel).

MacCauley other form of **MacAulay**

MacClean other form of **MacLean**

McCleary

Other form: **McCleery, McLeary, McLerie**

Scottish and Irish – occupational; from Gaelic meaning 'son of the clerk', referring to a clergyman.

MacClelland other form of **MacLellan**

McClintock other form of **McLintock**

McClure
Other forms: **McLure, McAleer**
Scottish – personal name; from Scottish Gaelic meaning 'son of the servant of Saint Odhar'. Many families of this name came from SW Scotland.

MacColl
Scottish – personal name; from Scottish Gaelic meaning 'son of **Coll**', an old personal name of obscure origin.

McConaghy other form of **McConnachie**

McConnachie
Other form: **McConaghy** (Irish)
Irish and Scottish – personal name; from Gaelic meaning 'son of **Duncan**'.

McConnell
Other form: **McConnel**
Scottish – personal name; from Scottish Gaelic meaning 'son of **Donald**'.

MacCormack
Other form: **McCormick**
Irish and Scottish – personal name; from Gaelic meaning 'son of **Cormack**'.

McCorquindale
Other form: **McCorquodale**
Scottish – personal name; from Scottish Gaelic meaning 'son' + the Old Norse name **Thorketill**, itself meaning 'Thor's kettle or cauldron'.

McCracken
Scottish and N Irish – personal name; of doubtful origin, possibly another form of **MacNaughton.** The name is first recorded in Galloway.

MacCrae other form of **MacRae**

MacCrimmon
Scottish – personal name; from Scottish Gaelic meaning 'son of **Ruimein**', the name deriving from an Old Norse name meaning 'fame' + 'protector'. The MacCrimmons were hereditary pipers to the chiefs of Clan Macleod.

MacCulloch

Other forms: **McCullagh**, **McCullough**

Scottish – nickname; of obscure origin, possibly from Gaelic meaning 'son of the boar'. It is first recorded in Galloway, whence many of the numerous Irish bearers may have crossed to N Ireland. There it may also derive from an Irish Gaelic name meaning 'son of the hound of Ulster'.

McDermott, **McDermid** other forms of **MacDiarmid**

MacDiarmid

Other forms: **McDermott**, **McDermid**

Irish and Scottish – personal name; from Gaelic meaning 'son of **Dermid**', the name of a legendary Irish hero. The name is common in Ireland, and also in Scotland. Many bearers there may be of Irish descent, but there are families of Scottish origin, in particular one originating in Glen Lyon in Perthshire; they are connected with Clan Campbell whose progenitor is claimed to be the Irish hero of the name.

MacDonald

Other form: **MacDonnell;** compare **McConnell**

Scottish and Irish – personal name; from Scottish Gaelic meaning 'son of **Donald**'. Clan Donald claims descent from the 12th-century Somerled who gained power over the Western Isles. MacDonald is the commonest clan name in Scotland and is also widely known in Ireland.

Macdoual other form of **MacDougall**.

MacDougall

Other forms: **MacDougal**, **McDoual**, **McDowall**, **McDowell**

Scottish and N Irish – personal name; from Scottish Gaelic meaning 'son of **Dougal**', itself meaning 'dark stranger'. Clan MacDougall in Argyll claim descent, like Clan Donald, from Somerled, Lord of the Isles in the 12th century. The form **McDowall** was prevalent in Galloway and from there many crossed to Ulster where the name is common.

MacDuff

Scottish – nickname; from Scottish Gaelic meaning 'son' + 'black, dark-haired'. There is no historical evidence for Macduff, the character in Shakespeare's *Macbeth*. Compare **Duff.**

MacEwan
Other form: **MacEwen**
Scottish – personal name; from Scottish Gaelic meaning 'son of
Ewan.

Macey other form of **Massey**

McFadden other form of **McFadyen**

McFadyen
Other forms: **McFadden, McFadzean**
Scottish and N Irish – personal name; from Gaelic meaning 'little
Pat'. The '-z-' in the second form is pronounced as '-y-'.

MacFall other form of **MacPhail**

MacFarlane
Other forms: **MacFarlan, McFarland, McParland**
Scottish and N Irish – personal name; from Gaelic meaning 'son of
Parlan', deriving from an Old Irish personal name often associated
with **Bartholomew**, though there is no evidence for any connection
between the names.

MacFaul other form of **MacPhail**

MacFee, MacFie other forms of **MacPhee**

MacGill
Other form: **Magill** (Irish)
Scottish and N Irish – nickname; from Gaelic meaning 'son of the
Lowlander or stranger'. The name was first recorded in Galloway;
from there it probably crossed to N Ireland, though the Irish name may
also come from several Irish names beginning with Giolla-. McGill
University in Montreal was orginally financed by James McGill
(1744–1813), a Scots-born Canadian fur-trader.

MacGillivray
Other form: **McGilvery**
Scottish – occupational; from Scottish Gaelic meaning 'son of the
servant of judgement'. The clan originated in Argyll.

MacGinnis other form of **MacInnes**

MacGloughlin other form of **MacLachlan**

MacGonagle
Other forms: **McGonagall, McGonigle,**
Irish – personal name; from Irish Gaelic meaning 'son of **Congail**'. It

is known in Scotland from William McGonagall (1830–1902), renowned for his bad verse which occasionally reaches comic heights.

MacGowan
Irish and Scottish – occupational; from Gaelic meaning 'son of the smith'.

McGrath
Irish [usually pronounced 'ma-**graa**] – personal name; of the same origin as **MacRae**.

MacGregor
Scottish – personal name; from Scottish Gaelic meaning 'son of **Gregor**'. The Clan Gregor was proscribed in 1603 because of their lawlessness, real or supposed, and many adopted other names. The 18th-century Rob Roy MacGregor, well known from Sir Walter Scott's novel, was known by his mother's name of Campbell.

McGuiness other form of MacInnes

Machin
Other forms: **Meacham, Meachin**
English – occupational; from Norman-French of Germanic origin meaning 'stonemason'.

MacInnes
Scottish – Other forms (Irish): **Maginnis, McGinnis, McGuiness**
Scottish and Irish – personal name; from Gaelic meaning 'son of **Angus**'.

MacIntosh
Other form: **Mackintosh**
Scottish – occupational; from Scottish Gaelic meaning 'son of the leader, chief'. Charles MacIntosh (1766–1843) invented a way of treating cloth with a rubber solution and thus gave his name to a form of waterproof clothing.

MacIntyre
Other forms: **McTear, McTier**
Scottish and Irish – occupational; from Scottish Gaelic meaning 'son of the carpenter'.

MacIver
Other form: **MacIvor**
Scottish – personal name; from Scottish Gaelic meaning 'son of **Ivor**'.

Mack
Scottish – personal name; probably from an Old Norse name. The name originates in SE Scotland and has no connection with the Highland clans.

Mackay [pronounced ma-**kye**]
Other form: **Mackie** [pronounced **mack**-y]
Scottish – personal name; from an Old Irish name **Aodh** (still used in Ireland). The Mackays are a Highland clan, associated mainly with the remote NW of Scotland. The Mackies are of Lowland origin.

Mackechnie
Scottish – personal name; from Scottish Gaelic meaning 'son of **Eacharn**', itself meaning 'horse lord'.

MacKellar
Scottish – personal name; from Scottish Gaelic meaning 'son of **Hilary**'.

Mackenzie
Scottish – personal name; from Scottish Gaelic meaning 'son of **Kenneth**'. The Mackenzies were a powerful clan in NW Scotland but lost influence after their support for the Jacobite risings in the 18th century. Alexander Mackenzie (1764–1820), a Scottish fur-trader and explorer, gave his name to the Mackenzie River in NW Canada.

Mackie other form of **Mackay**

MacKillop
Scottish – personal name; from Scottish Gaelic meaning 'son of **Philip**'.

MacKinlay
Scottish – personal name; from Scottish Gaelic meaning 'son of **Finlay**'.

MacKinnon
Scottish – personal name; from Scottish Gaelic meaning 'son' + an old Gaelic name meaning 'fair-born'. Several MacKinnons were abbots of Iona in the Middle Ages. The name is sometimes translated as **Love**, by confusion with another Gaelic name.

Mackintosh other form of **MacIntosh**

MacLachlan

Other forms: **McLaughlin**, **McLaughlan; McGloughlin** and **Mac Lachlainn** (Irish)

Scottish and Irish – personal name; from Gaelic meaning 'son of **Lachlan**'.

MacLaine other form of **MacLean**

MacLaren

Other form: **MacLaurin**

Scottish – personal name; from Scottish Gaelic meaning 'son of **Laurence**'. Colin MacLaurin (1698–1746) was a prominent mathematician of the Scottish Enlightenment.

McLaughlan, **McLaughlin** other forms of **MacLachlan**

MacLaurin other form of **MacLaren**

MacLay

Other form: **MacLeay**

Scottish – personal name; from Scottish Gaelic meaning 'son' + an old Gaelic name, itself meaning 'brown' + 'mountain'. Compare **Dunleavy.**

MacLean

[pronounced mac-**lane**]

Other forms: **MacLaine**, **MacClean**

Scottish and N Irish – personal name; from Gaelic meaning 'son of the servant of St John'. The Clan Maclean is based in the Isle of Mull.

McLeary other form of **McCleary**

MacLeay other form of **MacLay**

MacLellan

Other form: **MacLelland**, **MacClelland**

Scottish – personal name; from Scottish Gaelic meaning 'son of the servant of St Fillan', itself from Old Gaelic meaning 'wolf'. The name is first recorded in Galloway.

MacLennan

Scottish – personal name; from Scottish Gaelic meaning 'son of the servant of St Finnan', itself from Old Gaelic meaning 'white'.

MacLeod

Scottish – [pronounced ma-**cloud**] personal name; from an Old Norse name meaning 'ugly'. The Macleods were a large and powerful clan, with two main branches, of Skye and of Lewis.

McLerie other form of **McCleary**

McLintock
Other form: **McClintock**
Scottish and N Irish – personal name; from Scottish Gaelic meaning 'son of the servant of St Findan'.

McLure other form of **McClure**

Mac Mahon
Irish – personal name; anglicized form of Irish Gaelic **Mathghamhain**, itself meaning 'bear'.

MacMaster
Scottish – occupational; from Scottish Gaelic meaning 'son of the master' (referring to a clergyman).

MacMillan
Other form: **MacMullen** (N Irish)
Scottish and N Irish – occupational; from Gaelic meaning 'son of the tonsured man' (referring to a priest). The British Prime Minister Harold Macmillan (1894–1986) belonged to the publishing family of Macmillan, whose ancestors came from the island of Arran in the 19th century.

MacNab
Scottish – occupational; from Scottish Gaelic meaning 'son of the abbot'. The clan lands were in Perthshire in an area where there had been an important Celtic monastery.

McNair
1 Scottish – nickname; from Scottish Gaelic meaning either 'son of sallow-coloured **John**' or 'son of the heir',
2 Irish – occupational; from Irish Gaelic meaning 'son of the steward'.

MacNaughtan other form of **MacNaughton**

MacNaughton
Other form: **MacNaughtan**
Scottish and N Irish – personal name; from Scottish Gaelic meaning 'son of **Nechtan**', a Pictish name of obscure origin. (It was the name of several Pictish kings.)

MacNeil
Other form: **MacNeill**
Scottish – personal name; from Scottish Gaelic meaning 'son of **Neil**'. The clan has long connections with the island of Barra, where the

Chief, a wealthy American, restored the ancestral castle in the mid 20th century.

MacNicol

Scottish – personal name; from Scottish Gaelic meaning 'son of **Nicol**'.

McParland other form of MacFarlane

MacPhail

Other forms: **MacFall**, **MacFaul**

Scottish – personal name; from Scottish Gaelic meaning 'son of **Paul**'.

MacPhee

Other forms: **MacPhie**, **MacFee**, **MacFie**

Scottish – personal name; from Scottish Gaelic meaning 'son' + an Old Gaelic name meaning 'black ' + either 'peace' or 'fairy'.

MacPherson

Scottish – occupational; from Scottish Gaelic meaning 'son of the parson'. James MacPherson (1739–96) was a Scottish poet who published poems purporting to be translations of Ossian, a hero of ancient Irish legend.

MacPhie other form of MacPhee

MacQuarrie

Other forms: **MacQuarie**, **MacQuarry**

Scottish – personal name; from Scottish Gaelic meaning 'son of **Guaire**', itself an old Gaelic name meaning 'proud'. Lachlan MacQuarie (1761–1824), known as 'the Father of Australia', came from the island of Ulva, off Mull.

MacQueen

Scottish – personal name; from Scottish Gaelic meaning 'son' + an Old Gaelic name possibly meaning 'good-going'; or in some cases from an Old Norse name meaning 'servant'.

MacRae

Other form: **MacCrae**

Scottish – personal name; from on Old Gaelic first name meaning 'son of grace'. Compare **McGrath**.

MacRitchie see Ritchie

MacSorley

Scottish – personal name; from Scottish Gaelic meaning 'son of **Somerled**', itself an Old Norse name meaning 'summer wanderer'.

MacSporran
Scottish – occupational; from Scottish Gaelic meaning 'son of the purse' (probably from an ancestor who was a purse-bearer). The name is sometimes anglicized as **Purcell** or **Pursell.**

MacTaggart
Scottish – occupational; from Scottish Gaelic meaning 'son of the priest'.

MacTavish
Scottish – personal name; from Scottish Gaelic meaning 'son of **Tammas**', itself a Scots form of **Thomas.**

McTear, **McTier** Irish forms of **MacIntyre**

Madden
Other forms: **Maddigan**
Irish – personal name; anglicized form of Irish Gaelic **Ó Madain** from **O Madadhan**, descendant of **Madaidhín**, itself meaning 'hound'.

Madder
Other forms: **Maddern**, **Mather**
English
1 occupational; from Middle English meaning 'madder', a red dye from plant roots, referring to a dyer or seller of dyes.
2 nickname; from Middle English meaning 'madder', referring to someone with a rosy complexion.

Maddigan other form of **Madden**

Maddison
Other form: **Madison**
English – personal name; from Middle English **Madde**, itself a form of **Maud** or **Magdalen** meaning 'from Magdala'.

Madoc
Other forms: **Mattock**, **Maddocks**, **Maddox**
Welsh – personal name; from an Old Welsh name **Matoc**, meaning 'lucky'.

Magill other form of **MacGill**

Maginnis other form of **MacInnes**

Magnus
Other form: **Magnusson**
English – personal name; from a Scandinavian name **Magnús.**

Maher

Other form: **Meacher**

Irish – personal name; anglicized form of Irish Gaelic **Ó Meachair**, descendant of **Meachar**, itself meaning 'hospitable'.

Maidment

English – occupational; from Middle English meaning 'maiden' + 'man', referring to a servant whose employer was a woman, or a convent.

Mailer

Other forms: **Mayler**, **Maylor**

English

1 occupational; either from Middle English meaning 'mail', referring to the job of a maker of chain mail, or from Middle English meaning 'enameller'.

Welsh

2 personal name; from Old Welsh **Meilyr** meaning 'chief' + 'ruler'.

3 place name; from Maelor in Clywd, the name deriving from the personal name **Mael** + 'land'.

Mainwaring [pronounced 'mannering']

Other form: **Mannering**

English – place name; from an unknown place, the name deriving from Norman-French of Germanic origin meaning 'domain of **Warin**'.

Mair

Scottish – occupational; from Scots meaning 'a court official who executed legal writs etc', sometimes a hereditary appointment in medieval Scotland.

Maitland

Scottish and English – nickname/place name; of obscure origin, possibly from Old French meaning 'bad temper', though it may derive from a French place name. Maitlands were prominent in Scottish politics, including Sir Richard Maitland of Lethington (1496–1586) and his grandson John Maitland, Duke of Lauderdale (1616–82).

Major

English – personal name; from a Norman-French name of Germanic origin meaning 'council' + 'spear'. John Major (1943–) became prime minister of Britain in 1990.

Makin
Other forms: **Makinson, Meakin**
English
1 personal name; from a familiar form of **Matthew**.
2 nickname/occupational; from Middle English meaning 'maiden',
either referring to an effeminite man, or to a young servant girl.

Malcolm
Scottish – personal name; from the first name, itself from Scottish
Gaelic meaning '(tonsured) servant of St Columba'. Compare
MacCallum.

Malin
Other forms: **Malleson, Mallinson**
English – personal name; from **Mal(le)**, itself a familiar form of
Mary.

Mallard
English
1 personal name; from an Old French name **Malhard** from Norman-
French of Germanic origin meaning 'council' + 'brave'.
2 nickname; from Middle English meaning 'male wild duck', referring
to someone who resembled a duck.

Malleson other form of **Malin**

Mallinson other form of **Malin**

Mallon other form of **Malone**

Mallory
English – nickname; from French meaning 'unhappy, unlucky'.

Malloy other form of **Molloy**

Malone
Other form: **Mallon**
Irish – personal name; anglicized form of Irish Gaelic **Ó Maoil Eoin**,
'descendant of the servant of St John'.

Malthus
English – occupational; from Middle English meaning 'malthouse',
referring to someone who worked in a malthouse. Thomas Robert
Malthus (1766–1834) was an economist and author of an influential
work *Essay on the Principle of Population.*

Manion other form of **Mannin**

Manleigh other form of **Manley**

Manley

Other form: **Manleigh**

English – place name; from places in Cheshire and Devonshire, the name deriving from Old English meaning 'common, shared' + 'clearing'.

Mannering other form of **Mainwaring**

Manners

English – place name; from a place in Seine-Maritime in France, the name deriving from Latin meaning 'to reside'.

Mannin

Other form: **Manion**, **Manning**, **Mannion**

Irish – personal name; anglicized form of Irish Gaelic **Ó Mainnin**, 'descendant of **Mainnin**' itself probably meaning 'monk'.

Mannington other form of **Meriton**

Mannion other form of **Mannin**

Mansell

English

1 place name; from Le Mans in N France.

2 occupational; from Norman-French of Germanic origin meaning 'a feudal tenant who held land sufficient to support one family'.

Marchant

Other forms: **Marquand**, **Merchant**

English – occupational; from Middle English meaning 'trader, merchant'.

Marquand other form of **Marchant**

Marr

1 English – place name; from Marr in Yorkshire

2 Scottish – place name; from Mar in Aberdeenshire, itself of obscure origin.

Marriott

Other forms: **Marryat**, **Merriot**

English – personal name; from **Mariot**, a medieval form of **Mary.**

Marsden

English – place name; from places in Lancashire and Yorkshire, the name deriving from Old English meaning 'boundary' + 'valley'.

Marshall
Other forms: **Mascall, Maskall, Maskell, Maskill**
English and Scottish – occupational; from Middle English meaning 'marshall', itself from Norman-French of Germanic origin meaning 'horse servant'. It came to refer to a wide range of jobs from humble to high-status serving roles.

Marson other form of **Marston**

Marston
Other form: **Marson**
English – place name; from numerous places, the name deriving from Old English meaning 'marsh' + 'settlement'.

Martin
Other forms: **Martinson, Martyn**
English – personal name; from a Roman name **Martinus,** itself from the Latin name of the god of war.

Mascall, Maskall, Maskell, Maskill other forms of **Marshall**

Mason
English and Scottish – occupational; possibly from Old English meaning 'to make', referring to a builder, a worker in stone.

Massey
Other form: **Macey**
English – place name; from many places in northern France, the name deriving from a Gallo-Roman personal name **Maccius.**

Massinberd
Other form: **Massingbird**
English – nickname; from Middle English meaning 'brass' + 'beard', referring to someone with a golden-brown beard.

Matchett
N Irish – personal name; probably from a short form of **Matthew.**

Mather
English
1 occupational; from Old English meaning 'reaper, mower'.
2 occupational/nickname; other form of **Madder.**

Matheson
Other forms: **Mathieson, Mathison**
Scottish
1 personal name; meaning 'son of **Matthew**'.

2 nickname; from Gaelic meaning 'son of the bear'. Compare **Mac Mahon.**

Mathew other form of **Matthew**

Mathias other form of **Matthew**

Mathieson, Mathison other forms of **Matheson**

Matthew
Other forms: **Mathew, Mathias** (mainly Welsh), **Matheson** (Scottish), **Matthews, Matthewson, Mayhew**
English – personal name; from Hebrew meaning 'gift of God'.

Mattock other form of **Madoc**

Mattock other form of **Madoc**

Maudling
English – personal name; from the Middle English name **Maudeleyn**, itself from Hebrew meaning 'woman from Magdala'.

Maugham other form of **Maughan**

Maughan
Other form: **Maugham**
I 1rish – personal name; anglicized form of Irish Gaelic **Ó Mocháin**, descendant of **Mochán**, itself meaning 'early'.
2 Welsh – place name; from places in Monmouth, the name deriving either from the Church of St Maughan, or else from Welsh meaning 'the place of Cain'. William Somerset Maugham (1874–1965) was a British writer, master of the short story.

Maurice other form of **Morris**

Maxwell
Scottish – place name; from a pool in the River Tweed, the name deriving from an Old English personal name + Old English meaning 'pool'. The Maxwells were a powerful family in S Scotland in times past.

Mayhew other form of **Matthew**

Mayler, Maylor other forms of **Mailer**

Maynall other form of **Meynell**

Maynell other form of **Meynell**

Meacham other form of **Machin**

Meacher other form of **Maher**

Meachin other form of **Machin**

Meakin other form of **Makin**

Meaney
Other form: **Mooney**
Irish – personal name; anglicized form of Irish Gaelic **Ó Maonaigh**, descendant of **Maonach**, itself meaning 'rich'.

Medhurst other form of **Midhurst**

Meiklejohn
Scottish – nickname; from Scots meaning 'big John' (referring to the taller or elder of two men of the same name).

Meldrum
Scottish – place name; from the lands in Aberdeenshire, the name deriving from Old Gaelic meaning 'noble' + 'ridge'.

Melling
English – place name; from places in Lancashire, the name deriving from an Old English tribal name meaning 'people of **Mealla**'.

Mellor
English – place name; from places in Derbyshire, Lancashire and Yorkshire, the name deriving from Old Welsh meaning 'bare' + 'hill'.

Melrose
Scottish – place name; the town in Roxburghshire, the name probably deriving from Old Welsh meaning 'bare' + moor'.

Melville
Other form: **Melvin**
Scottish – place name; from several places in Normandy called Malleville, the name deriving from French meaning 'bad' + settlement'. Andrew Melville (1545-c.1622) was a Scottish Protestant reformer and educator. The American novelist Herman Melville (1819–91) was of Scottish descent.

Menzies
Scottish [in Scotland usually pronounced **ming**-is, though this is giving way to the spelling pronunciation of **men**-ziz]
place name; variant of **Manners.** Of Norman-French origin, the Menzies family gained power in Perthshire, where Castle Menzies has recently been restored.

Mercer
English – occupational; from Old French meaning 'trader', referring especially to one who dealt in fine fabrics.

Merchant other form of **Marchant**

Meredith

Other forms: **Merriday, Merridew**

Welsh – personal name; from a Welsh name **Meredydd** or **Maredudd**, itself from Old Welsh probably meaning 'splendour' + 'lord'.

Meriton

Other forms: **Merrington, Mirrington, Mannington, Morrington**

English – place name; from places in Shropshire and Durham, the name deriving in the case of the Shropshire place from Old English meaning 'pleasant' + 'hill' and the Durham one probably from an Old English name **Maera** + 'settlement'.

Merriday other form of **Meredith**

Merridew other form of **Meredith**

Merrington other form of **Meriton**

Merriot other form of **Marriott**

Merton

English – place name; from numerous places, the name deriving from Old English meaning 'lake' + 'settlement'. Paul Merton is an English comic actor and popular TV performer in the 1990s.

Meynell

Other forms: **Maynell, Maynall**

English

1 place name; from many small places in France, the name deriving from a diminutive of Middle English meaning 'dwelling', referring usually to an isolated house occupied by a landlord.

2 personal name; from Norman-French of Germanic origin meaning 'strength' + 'battle'.

Michael

Other forms: **Michaelson, Miggles**

English – personal name; from the first name, itself from Hebrew (via Greek), meaning 'Who is like the Lord?'.

Michelson other form of **Mitchell**

Michie

Scottish – [pronounced '**mikh**-i'] personal name; from a familiar form of **Michael.** The name originates in NE Scotland and the Michies are said to be descended from a Michael MacDonald who settled in Aberdeenshire in the16th century.

Middlemas

Other form: **Middlemiss**

Scottish – place name; from an area in Roxburghshire, the name deriving from Older Scots meaning 'middle(most)'.

Midhurst

Other form: **Medhurst**

English – place name; from a place in Sussex, the name deriving from Old English meaning 'amongst' + 'wooded hill'.

Miggles other form of **Michael**

Miles

Other forms: **Milsom**, **Milson**, **Myles**

English – personal name; from a name **Milo**, itself from Norman-French of Germanic origin, perhaps meaning 'mercy'.

Mill

Other forms: **Mills**, **Milne** (Scottish)

English and Scottish – place name/occupational; from Middle English meaning 'mill', referring either to someone who lived near a mill, or to someone who worked in one.

Millar other form of **Miller**

Miller

Other forms: **Millar**, **Milner**

English – occupational; from Old English meaning 'miller'.

Millership other form of **Millichamp**

Millican other form of **Milligan**

Millichamp

Other forms: **Millership**, **Millichap**

English – place name; from a place in Shropshire, the name deriving from Old English meaning 'mill' + 'hill' + 'closed valley'.

Milligan

Other forms: **Millican**, **Mulligan**

Irish – personal name; anglicized form of Irish Gaelic **Ó Maolagáin**, descendant of **Maolagán**, itself meaning 'bald'.

Mills other form of **Mill**

Milne Scottish form of **Mill**

Milner other form of **Miller**

Milsom other form of **Miles**

Milson other form of **Miles**

Milton

English – place name; from many places, the name deriving in most cases from Old English meaning 'middle' + 'settlement', but a few may derive from Old English 'mill' + 'settlement'. John Milton (1608–74) was an English poet.

Minett other form of **Mynott**

Minnock other form of **Minogue**

Minogue

Other form: **Minnock**

Irish – personal name; anglicized form of Irish Gaelic **Ó Muineog**, descendant of **Muineog**, itself meaning 'monk'.

Minshull

English – place name; from places in Cheshire, the name deriving from an Old English name **Mann** + 'shelf, ledge'.

Mirrington other form of **Meriton**

Mitchell

Other forms: **Michelson**, **Mitchelson**

English, Scottish and Irish – personal name; from Old French **Michel**, itself a form of **Michael.**

Mockridge other form of **Muggeridge**

Moffat

Other form: **Moffet**

Scottish and N Irish – place name; from the town in Dumfries-shire, the name probably deriving from Scottish Gaelic meaning 'field' + 'long'.

Mogridge other form of **Muggeridge**

Moir

Scottish – nickname; from Scottish Gaelic meaning 'big'. The name is common in NE Scotland.

Molloy

Other forms: **Malloy**, **Mulloy**

Irish – personal name; anglicized forms from the following Irish Gaelic names: **Ó Maolmhuaidh**, descendant of **Maolmaidhuadh**, itself meaning 'chieftain' + 'proud'; **Ó Maol Aodha**, descendant of the devotee of **Aodh**; **Ó Maol Mhaodhóg**, descendant of the devotee of **Maodhóg**.

Moncrieff [usually pronounced 'mon-**creef**']
Other forms: **Moncreif**, **Moncrieffe**
Scottish – place name; from the place in Perthshire, the name deriving
from Scottish Gaelic meaning 'hill' + 'tree'.

Monro, **Monroe** other forms of **Munro**

Montgomerie other form of **Montgomery**

Montgomery
Other form: **Montgomerie**
English, Scottish and N Irish – place name; from a place in Normandy,
the name deriving from French meaning 'hill' + a Germanic name
meaning 'man' + 'power'. The family held lands in England from the
time of the Norman Conquest and in Scotland from the 12th century.
A branch of the Scottish family moved to Donegal and from them was
descended Viscount Montgomery of Alamein (1887–1976), the
Second World War military leader.

Moodie other form of **Moody**

Moody
Other form: **Moodie**
English – nickname; from Middle English meaning 'haughty, angry',
referring to an arrogant or foolhardy person.

Mooney other form of **Meaney**

Moorcock other form of **Moore**

Moore
Other forms: **More**, **Muir**, **Mure** (Scottish), **Moorcock**, **Morrell**
1 English and Scottish – place name; from many places, the name
deriving from Middle English meaning 'moor, fen'.
2 English – nickname; from Old French meaning 'Moor, Negro',
referring to someone with a dark complexion.
3 English – personal name; from a name of the same origin as 2.
4 Irish – personal name; anglicized form of Irish Gaelic **Ó Mórdha**,
descendant of **Mórdha**, itself meaning 'proud, great'.
5 Welsh and Scottish – nickname; from Scottish Gaelic and Welsh
meaning 'big'.

Morgan
Welsh, Scottish and Irish – personal name; from an Old Welsh
personal name, itself meaning 'sea' + 'bright'.

Morison other form of **Morrison**

Morrell other form of **Moore**

Morrice other form of **Morris**

Morrington other form of **Meriton**

Morris
Other forms: **Maurice, Morrice, Morrish, Morse**
English, Welsh, Scottish and Irish – personal name; from the first name, itself from Latin meaning 'Moorish, dark-skinned'. See also **Morrison.**

Morrison
Other forms: **Morison, Murison**
1 English and Scottish – personal name; meaning 'son of **Morris.**
2 Scottish – personal name; from Scottish Gaelic meaning 'son of the servant of Mary'.

Morrissey
Irish – personal name; anglicized form of Irish Gaelic **Ó Muirgheas**, descendant of **Muirgheasa**, itself meaning 'sea' + 'taboo'.

Morse other form of **Morris**

Mouat other form of **Mowat**

Mowat
Other forms: **Mouat, Mowatt**
Scottish and N English – place name; from Norman French meaning 'hill' + 'high'.

Muggeridge
Other forms: **Mockridge, Mogridge**
English – place name; from Devonshire, the name deriving from an Old English name **Mogga** + 'ridge'.

Muir Scottish form of **Moore**

Mullally
Other form: **Lally**
Irish – personal name; from Irish Gaelic **Ó Maolalaidh**, descendant of **Maolaladh**, itself meaning 'chieftain' + 'speckled'.

Mulligan other form of **Milligan**

Mulloy other form of **Molloy**

Mulrine
Other form: **Mulryan**
Irish – personal name; anglicized form of Irish Gaelic **O Maoil Riain**, descendant of **Maol Riain**, itself meaning 'servant of St **Ryan**'.

Mulroy

Irish – personal name; anglicized form of Irish Gaelic **Ó Maolruaidh**, descendant of **Maolruadh**, itself meaning 'chief' + 'red'.

Mulryan other form of **Mulrine**.

Munro [in Scotland usually pronounced mun-**row**]
Other forms: **Monro(e)**, **Munrow**
Scottish – place name; probably from Gaelic meaning 'mouth of the River Ro' (in N Ireland). The clan has been based in Easter Ross since at least the 14th century. James Monroe (1758–1831), 5th President of the USA, was of Scottish descent. Mountains in Scotland over 3 000 feet (914 metres) are called Munros, after Sir Hugh T Munro who first listed them in 1891.

Murdoch [in Scotland, -ch pronounced as in 'loch']
Other form: **Murdock**
Scottish – personal name; from a Scottish Gaelic name meaning 'sea' + 'warrior'. William Murdock (1754–1839) was a Scottish engineer, pioneer of gas lighting. Iris Murdoch (1919–), novelist, is of Irish origin.

Mure Scottish form of **Moore**

Murison other form of **Morrison**

Murphy

Irish – personal name; anglicized form of Irish Gaelic **Ó Murchadha**, descendant of **Murchadh**, itself meaning 'sea' + 'warrior'.

Murray

Scottish – place name; from the area (Moray) in NE Scotland, the name deriving from Old Gaelic meaning 'sea' + 'settlement'. It is the family name of the Dukes of Atholl. Les Murray (1938–) is an Australian poet of Scottish descent.

Musgrave

English – place name; from villages in Cumberland, the name deriving from Old English meaning 'mouse' + 'grove'.

Myles other form of **Miles**

Mynett other form of **Mynott**

Mynott

Other forms: **Minett**, **Mynett**
English – nickname; from Old French meaning 'dainty, pleasing'.

N

Naghten other form of **Naughton**

Naismith
Other form: **Nasmith**
Scottish and English – occupational; from Old English meaning 'knife or nail' + 'smith'.

Nancarrow
Cornish – place name; from Cornish meaning 'stag' + 'valley'.

Napier
Scottish and English – occupational; referring to a person who sold linen, or looked after the table linen in a large household. John Napier of Merchiston (1550–1617) was a mathematician and the inventor of logarithms. (His home is now occupied by Napier University of Edinburgh).

Nash
Other form: **Nashe**
English – place name; from Middle English meaning 'ash tree'.

Nasmith other form of **Naismith**

Naughton
Other forms: **Knockton, Naghten, Norton** (Irish)
1 Irish – personal name; anglicized form of Irish Gaelic **Neachtan**, itself from the name of the god of water.
2 English – place name; from a place in Suffolk, the name deriving from Old English meaning 'navel, depression' + 'enclosure'.

Neal, Neale, Neall other forms of **Neil**

Neave
Other forms: **Neeve, Neve**
English – nickname; from Middle English meaning 'nephew', used to refer to a relative, but also commonly a nickname for a spendthrift or sponger.

Needham
English – place name; from places in Derbyshire, Norfolk and Suffolk, the name deriving from Old English meaning 'poverty, need' + 'homestead'.

Neeve other form of **Neave**

Negus

English – place name; probably from Old English meaning 'near' + 'house', suggesting somewhere near, but not actually part of a settlement. Arthur George Negus (1903–85) was an English broadcaster and antiques expert.

Neil

Other forms: **Neal(e)**, **Neall**, **Neill**, **Neilson**, **O Neil**

Irish and Scottish – personal name; of uncertain origin, possibly from Gaelic meaning 'champion'. See also **MacNeil.**

Nelson

English – personal name; from either the name **Nell** or **Neil** + 'son'.

Nesbit, **Nesbitt** other forms of **Nisbit**

Neve other form of **Neave**

Neven other form of **Niven**

Neville

Other form: **Newell**

1 English – place name; from places in France, the name deriving from Old French meaning 'new' + 'settlement'.

2 Irish – personal name; anglicized form of Irish Gaelic **Ó Niadh**, itself meaning 'warrior'.

Nevin other form of **Niven**

Newbold

English – nickname; from Old English meaning 'new' + 'building', referring to someone who lived in a new house.

Newcomb

Other form: **Newcome**

English – nickname; from Old English meaning 'new' + 'come', referring to a newly-arrived person in the area.

Newell other form of **Neville**

Newman

Other form: **Nyman**

English – nickname; from Old English meaning 'new settler'.

Nichol, **Nicholson**, **Nickal**, **Nickelson**, **Nicolson** other forms of **Nicolas**

Nickson other form of **Nixon**

Nicolas
Other forms: **Nicolson, Nichol, Nichols, Nicholson, Nickal, Nickelson**
English – personal name; from the first name, itself from Greek meaning 'victory' + 'people'.

Nimmo
Scottish – Although several fanciful theories have been put forward, the origin of this name remains obscure.

Nisbet
Other forms: **Nisbett, Nesbit, Nesbitt**
Scottish and N English – place name; from several places of this name, deriving from Old English meaning 'nose' + either 'piece of land' (referring to a nose-shaped piece of raised ground) or 'bend' (referring to a sharp bend in a river).

Niven
Other forms: **Neven, Nevin**
Scottish – personal name; from an old Gaelic first name, meaning 'little saint', once common in SW Scotland.

Nixon
Other form: **Nickson**
English, Northern Irish and Scottish – personal name; from a Middle English short form of **Nicholas.**

Noakes other form of **Oakes**

Nock other form of **Oakes**

Noel
Other form: **Nowell**
English – personal name; from the first name, itself from Old French meaning 'Christmas'.

Nolan
Other forms: **Nowlan, Noland**
Irish – personal name; anglicized form of Irish Gaelic **Ó Nualláin**, 'descendant of **Nuallán**, itself meaning 'noble, famous'.

Norcott other form of **Northcote**

Norman
English – personal name; from the first name, itself from Germanic meaning 'north' + 'man'.

Norrie other form of **Norris**

Norris
Other forms: **Norrie** (Scottish), **Norrish**, **Nurse**
English and Scottish
1 nickname; from Old French meaning 'northener', referring to someone who had come from the north to settle further south.
2 place name; from Old English meaning 'north' + 'house'.
3 occupational; from Old French meaning 'wet nurse', referring to someone who acted as a foster mother or nurse.

Northcote other form of **Northcott**

Northcott
Other forms: **Norcott**, **Northcote**
English – place name; from places in Devonshire and Herefordshire, the name deriving from Old English meaning 'north' + 'dwelling'.

Norton
1 English – place name; from numerous places, the name deriving from Old English meaning 'north' + 'settlement'.
2 Irish – personal name; other form of **Naughton.**

Nott
Other form: **Notting**
English – nickname; from Middle English meaning 'bald', referring to someone with very short hair, or bald.

Nowell other form of **Noel**

Nowlan other form of **Nolan**

Noy
Other forms: **Noyce**, **Noyes**
English – personal name; from the name **Noah**, itself from Hebrew of uncertain meaning, perhaps meaning 'comfort' or 'long-lived'.

Nunn
English – nickname; from Middle English meaning 'nun', referring to someone who was very devout, or to someone who worked at a convent.

Nurse other form of **Norris**

Nuthall other form of **Nuttall**

Nuttall
Other form: **Nuthall**
English – place name; from various places, notably one in Lancashire, the name deriving from Old English meaning 'nut' + 'hill', or, in some cases, 'nut' + 'nook or recess'.

Nye
English – place name; from Middle English meaning either 'at the river' or 'at the island'.

Nyeland
English – place name; from places in Dorset and Somerset, the name deriving from Old English meaning 'at the island'.

Nyman other form of **Newman**

O

Oak, **Oake** other forms of **Oakes**

Oakden
Other forms: **Ogden**, **Ogdon**
English – place name; from places in Lancashire, the name deriving from Old English meaning 'oak' + 'valley'. John Andrew Howard Ogdon (1937–89) was an English pianist and composer.

Oakeley other form of **Oakley**

Oakes
Other forms: **Noakes**, **Nock**, **Oak**, **Oake**
English – place name; from Old English meaning 'of, at' + 'oaks'.

Oakley
Other forms: **Ogley**, **Oakeley**, **Ok(e)ly**
English – place name; from numerous places, the name deriving from Old English meaning 'oak' + 'wood, clearing'.

Oates
Other forms: **Oddy**, **Oddie**
English – personal name; from Norman-French of Germanic origin meaning 'riches'.

Oatley
English – place name; from a place in Shropshire, the name deriving from Old English meaning 'oats' + 'clearing, field'.

O Brien other form of **Brian**

O Byrne other form of **Byrne**

O Casey other form of **Casey**

O Connell other form of **Connell**

O Connor other form of **Connor**

Oddie other form of **Oates**

Oddy other form of **Oates**

Odell
English – place name; from a place in Bedfordshire, the name deriving from Old English meaning 'woad' + 'hill'.

O Donnell other form of **Donald**

O Donovan other form of **Donovan**

O Farrall other form of **Farrell**

O Farrelly other form of **Farrell**

O Ferrally other form of **Farrell**

O Ferrell other form of **Ferrell**

O Gallagher other form of **Gallagher**

Ogden, **Ogdon** other forms of **Oakden**

Ogilvie
Other form: **Ogilvy**
Scottish – place name; from the area in Angus, the name of obscure origin, possibly from Old Welsh meaning 'high plain'. It is the family name of the Earls of Airlie.

Ogley other form of **Oakley**

O Grady other form of **Grady**

Okeley, **Okley** other form of **Oakley**

Oldbury
English – place name; from several places, the name deriving from Old English meaning 'old' + 'fort', referring to a pre-Anglo-Saxon settlement.

Oldroyd
English – place name; from Old English meaning 'old' + Yorkshire dialect meaning 'clearing'.

Ollerenshaw
English – place name; from a place in Derbyshire, the name deriving from Old English meaning 'alders' + 'copse, thicket'.

O Neil other form of **Neil**

Onions
English – personal name; from Old French meaning 'son of **Ennion**'.

Openshaw
English – place name; from a place in Lancashire, the name deriving from Old English meaning 'unenclosed' + 'copse, thicket'.

Orde
English – place name; from a place in Northumberland, the name deriving from Old English meaning 'spear', referring to a projecting piece of land.

O Regan other form of **Regan**

Orledge

English – Other form: **Orlich**

occupational; from Old French meaning 'clock', referring to a clockmaker.

Orr

Scottish – nickname; from Scottish Gaelic meaning 'dun-coloured'.

Orrell

English – place name; from places in Lancashire, the name deriving from Old English meaning 'ore' +'hill'.

Orton other form of **Overton**

O Ryan other form of **Ryan**

Osborne

Other forms: **Osbourne, Osburn, Usborne**

English – personal name; from an Old English name, itself probably from Old Norse meaning 'god' + 'bear'.

Ovens

English – place name; from Old English meaning 'at the furnace'.

Overton

Other form: **Orton**

English – place name; from many places, the name deriving from Old English meaning 'riverbank, slope' + 'settlement'.

Owen

Other form: **Owens**

Welsh – personal name; from the first name, itself a Welsh translation from Latin meaning 'well-born'. Robert Owen (1771–1858) was a social reformer, founder of the village of New Lanark.

P

Packer

English – occupational; from Middle English meaning 'to pack', referring to someone who packed wool.

Padley

English – place name; from a place in Derbyshire, the name deriving from Old English meaning 'frog, toad' + 'clearing'.

Page

Other form: **Paget**, **Paige**

English – occupational; from Middle English meaning 'page, young servant'.

Pailthorpe

Other form: **Palethorpe**

English – place name; from a place in Yorkshire, the name deriving from Old English meaning 'frog, toad' + 'farm'.

Paine

Other forms: **Pane**, **Payne**

English – personal name; from the Middle English name **Paine**, itself from Latin meaning 'countryman'.

Paisley

Scottish – place name; from the town in Renfrewshire, the name deriving from Latin (via Gaelic or Old Welsh) meaning 'church'. Ian Paisley (1926–) is a Northern Ireland politician and clergyman.

Palethorpe other form of **Pailthorpe**

Palfrey

Other form: **Palfreyman**

English – occupational; from Middle English meaning 'saddle horse' referring to someone who dealt in, or looked after, saddle horses.

Pallant

English – place name; from a district of Chichester where the archbishop had special rights, the name deriving from Old English meaning 'palace, enclosure'.

Pallis other form of **Palliser**

Palliser

Other forms: **Pallis**, **Pallister**, **Palser**

English – occupational; from Old French meaning 'palisade', referring to a maker of fences.

Palmer

English – nickname; from Middle English meaning 'palm tree', referring to a pilgrim to the Holy Land. Such travellers brought back palms as proof that they had been there.

Palser other form of **Palliser**

Pane other form of **Paine**

Pankhurst

English – place name; from Pankhurst or Pinkhurst in Sussex, the name deriving from Pentecost, that is Whitsuntide, meaning 'fiftieth day' (after Easter). As Pentecost also exists as a rare surname, there is some doubt which came first, the place name or the surname.
Emmeline Pankhurst (1857–1928) was a suffragette, as were her daughters Sylvia and Christabel.

Papworth

English – personal name; from an Old English name **Papa +** 'enclosure'.

Pardew other form of **Pardoe**

Pardner

Other form: **Partner**

English – occupational; from Middle English meaning 'licensed seller of indulgences' (a method of gaining remission from punishment for sins).

Pardoe

Other forms: **Pardew**, **Pardy**, **Purdy**, **Perdue**

English – nickname; from French meaning 'by God' (a common oath in the Middle Ages), referring to a frequent user of the phrase.

Pargetter

Other form: **Pargiter**

English – occupational; from Old French meaning 'plasterer'.

Paris

Other forms: **Parris**, **Parrish**

English – place name; from the name of the French capital, the name deriving from the name of the Parisii tribe.

Parkin

Other forms: **Parkins, Parkinson, Parkyn, Perkins, Purkins**

English – personal name; from a medieval name **Perkin**, itself a familiar form of **Peter**.

Parley

English – place name; from Old English meaning 'pear' + 'wood, clearing'.

Parmenter

Other form: **Parminter**

English – occupational; from Old French meaning 'tailor'.

Parnall

Other forms: **Parnell, Parnwell**

English – personal name; from the medieval female name **Parnell**, itself from a Latin name **Petronilla.**

Parr

English – place name; from a place in Lancashire, the name deriving from Old English meaning 'enclosure'. Catherine Parr (1512–48) was the sixth wife of King Henry Vlll.

Parris, Parrish other form of Paris

Parry

Other forms: **Barry, Pendry**

Welsh – personal name; from Welsh 'ap' meaning 'son of' + **Harry.**

Partner other form of Pardner

Pascall

Other form: **Pascoe**

English – personal name; from the medieval name **Pascal**, itself from French based on the Hebrew word for Easter.

Pasmore other form of Passmore

Passmore

Other form: **Pasmore**

English – nickname; from Middle English meaning 'to go across the marsh', or from the Norman-French surname **Passemer** meaning 'to go across the sea'.

Pate

Other forms: **Patey, Paton**

English – personal name; from a familiar form of **Patrick.**

Paterson

Other form: **Patterson**

Scottish – personal name; meaning 'son of **Patrick**' William Paterson (1658–1719) was a Scottish financier and the founder of Bank of England.

Patey other form of **Pate**

Paton other form of **Pate**

Patrick

Other form: **Fitzpatrick**

English – personal name; from the first name, itself from Irish Gaelic **Pádraig**, probably from Latin **Patricius** meaning 'noble man'.

Patterson other form of **Paterson**

Paul

Other forms: **Paulle**, **Paulson**, **Pole**, **Polson**, **Powell**

English – personal name; from the first name, itself from Latin meaning 'small'.

Paxton

English and Scottish – place name; from places in Cambridgeshire and in Berwickshire, the name deriving from an Old English name + 'settlement'.

Payne other form of **Paine**

Peach

English – occupational/nickname; possibly from the name of the fruit (which was known in England in the Middle Ages), referring to a grower or seller of peaches. More frequently, the name is likely to be a corruption of French meaning 'sin', applied to a wrongdoer.

Peagram other form of **Pilgrim**

Pearce

Other forms: **Pears**, **Pearson**, **Pierce**, **Piers**,

English – personal name; from the Middle English name **Piers**, itself a form of **Peter**.

Peasey other form of **Pusey**

Peckham

English – place name; from places in London and Kent, the name deriving from Old English meaning 'hill' + 'homestead'.

Peden

Scottish – personal name; from a familiar form of **Patrick**.

Peebles
Scottish – place name; from the town to the south of Edinburgh or from lands in Angus, the name deriving from Old Welsh meaning 'tent, pavilion'.

Peel
English – nickname; from Norman-French meaning 'pole or stake', referring to a tall thin person.

Pelham
English – place name; from a place in Hertfordshire, the name deriving from an Old English personal name **Peotla** + 'settlement'.

Pemberton
English – place name; from a place in Greater Manchester, the name deriving from Old English meaning 'barley' + 'enclosure'.

Pender other form of **Pinder**

Pendle
English – place name; from a place in Lancashire and an element in many other names, the name deriving from Old Welsh meaning 'hill' + Old English also meaning 'hill'.

Pendleton
English – place name; from a place in Lancashire, the name deriving from Old Welsh meaning 'hill' + Old English also meaning 'hill' + 'settlement'.

Pendreich, **Pendrigh** shortened forms of **Pittendreigh**

Pendry other form of **Parry**

Penicuik other form of **Pennycuik**

Penman
Scottish – place name; probably deriving from Old Welsh meaning 'hill' + 'stone'; it is found as an element of several Border place names.

Pennington
English – place name; from places in Hampshire and Lancashire, the name deriving from Old English meaning 'penny' + 'settlement, farm', referring to one whose tenant paid a penny rent.

Pennycuik
Other forms: **Pennycook**, **Pennycuick**, **Penicuik**
Scottish – place name; from the town in Midlothian, the name probably deriving from Old Welsh meaning 'hill' + 'cuckoo'.

Pennyfather other form of **Pennyfeather**

Pennyfeather
Other form: **Pennyfather**
English – nickname; from Old English meaning 'penny' + 'father', referring to a miser.

Penrose
Cornish – place name; from places in Cornwall and Devon, the name deriving from Cornish meaning 'head, top' + 'heath'.

Pentreath
Cornish – place name; from Cornish meaning 'head, top' + 'ferry, beach'.

Pentrose
Cornish and Welsh – place name; from places in Cornwall and Wales, the name deriving from Celtic meaning 'head, top' + 'shore'.

Pepys
English [pronounced peeps]
personal name; from the Norman-French name **Pepis**, probably meaning 'awe-inspiring'. Samuel Pepys (1633–1703) was an English diarist and Admiralty official.

Perceval other form of **Percival**

Percival
Other form: **Perceval**
English
1 personal name; from the first name which was invented by the medieval poet, Chrétien de Troyes, for a character who was supposed to be one of King Arthur's knights.
2 place name; see **Percy.**

Percy
English – place name; from a place in Calvados, France, the name deriving from a Latin name **Persius.**

Perdue other form of **Pardoe**

Perkins other form of **Parkin**

Peter
Other forms: **Peters**, **Peterson**, **Petrie** (Scottish)
English – personal name; from the first name, itself from Greek meaning 'rock'.

Petrie Scottish form of **Peter**

Pett other form of **Pitt**

Pettifer
Other form: **Pettiford**
English – nickname; from Old French meaning 'foot' + 'iron',
referring to someone with an artificial limb, or else to a strong walker.

Pettigrew
Scottish – nickname; of obscure origin but possibly a jocular name for
a small person, from Old French meaning 'small' + 'growth'.

Petts other form of **Pitt**

Pewsey other form of **Pusey**

Peyton
English – place name; from an Old English personal name **Paega** +
'settlement'.

Phair other form of **Fair**

Pharoah other form of **Farrar**

Phayre other form of **Fair**

Pheasey other form of **Vaisey**

Phelps other form of **Phillips**

Philcox other form of **Phillips**

Philip, **Philips** other forms of **Phillips**

Phillips
Other forms: **Phelps, Philcox, Philip(s), Philpot, Philpotts**
English – personal name; from the Greek name **Philippos**, itself from
Greek meaning 'lover of horses'.

Phoenix other form of **Fenwick**

Pickard
English – place name; from Picardy in N France, the name deriving
from Old French.

Pickavance
English – nickname; from Old French meaning 'prick, spur' +
'forward', referring to a fast horseman.

Pickering
English – place name; from a place in Yorkshire, the name deriving
from the Old English tribe name Picoringas, meaning 'the people on
the ridge'.

Pickett other form of **Piggot**

Pickles
English – place name; from Middle English meaning 'paddock'.

Picton
English – place name; from places in Cheshire and Yorkshire, the name deriving from Old English meaning 'peak' + 'settlement', or from a personal name **Pica**, itself from Old English meaning 'sharp, pointed peak'.

Pierce other form of **Pearce**

Pierpont other form of **Pierrepoint**

Pierrepoint
Other form: **Pierpont**
English – place name; from places in Normandy, the name deriving from Old French meaning 'stone' + 'bridge'.

Piers other form of **Pearce**

Piggot
Other form: **Pickett**, **Piggott**
English – personal name; from the familiar form of the name **Pica**, itself from Old English meaning 'sharp, pointed peak'.

Pike
Other form: **Pyke**
English
1 personal name; from a name **Pica**, itself from Old English meaning 'sharp, pointed peak'.
2 nickname; from Old French meaning 'woodpecker' or from Old English meaning 'sharp, pointed peak', referring to someone with a beaky nose or tall and thin, like a pike.
3 occupational; from Old English meaning 'sharp, pointed peak' which through Middle English gave rise to 'pike' as the name of the fish with the sharp snout, and also for the long pointed weapon. The name refers to a fisherman, a soldier who used a pike, or a workman using a digging tool.

Pilgrim
Other form: **Peagram**
English – nickname; for someone who had made a pilgrimage to the Holy Land.

Pillinger
English – occupational; from Old French meaning 'baker'.

Pim other form of **Pymm**

Pinder
Other form: **Pender**
Scottish and English – occupational; from Middle English meaning 'impounder of cattle' or 'person who distrains a debtor's goods'.

Pinfold
English – occupational; from Old English meaning 'pound, pen', referring to a person in charge of herding cattle into a pound.

Pinkerton
Scottish – place name; from the lands in East Lothian, the name of obscure origin (the last element from Old English meaning 'settlement').

Pirie
Other form: **Pirrie**
Scottish – personal name; probably from a familiar form of **Peter** (based on French **Pierre**). The name is common in NE Scotland.

Pitcairn [in Scotland usually pronounced pit-**cairn**]
Scottish – place name; from the lands in Fife, the name deriving from Old Welsh meaning 'settlement' + Scottish Gaelic meaning 'hill, heap of stones'.

Pitman other form of **Pitt**

Pitney
English – place name; from a place in Somerset, the name deriving from an Old English name **Pytta** or **Peota** + 'island'.

Pitt
Other forms: **Pett(s)**, **Pitman**
English – place name; from places in Hampshire or Sussex, the name deriving from Old English meaning 'pit'. William Pitt (1759–1806) was a British prime minister.

Pittendreigh
Other forms: **Pendreich**, **Pendrigh**
Scottish – place name; from several places of this name, deriving from Old Welsh meaning 'settlement' + Old Gaelic meaning 'face, aspect'.

Pizzey, Pizzie other form of **Pusey**

Platt
English
1 nickname; from Old French meaning 'flat', referring to a thin person.

2 place name; from a place in Lancashire, the name deriving from Old French meaning 'flat', suggesting flat land or a plank bridge.

Plenderleith
Scottish – place name; from the place in Roxburghshire, the name of obscure origin.

Plewis other form of **Plews**

Plews
Other form: **Plewis**
English – place name; from Old English meaning 'at the plough (land)', a term referring to an area able to be ploughed by a team of eight oxen.

Plimmer other form of **Plummer**

Plomley other form of **Plumley**

Plowden
English – place name; from a place in Shropshire, the name deriving from Old English meaning 'play' + 'valley'.

Plowwright
English – occupational; from Old English meaning 'plough maker'.

Plumley
Other form: **Plomley**
English – place name; from many places, including one in Cheshire, the name deriving from Old English meaning 'plum' + 'clearing'.

Plummer
Other form: **Plimmer**
English – occupational; from Old French meaning 'plumber, worker in lead'.

Poindexter
English – nickname; from Old French meaning 'fist' + 'right', probably referring to a skilled fighter.

Pole
English
1 place name; from Old English meaning 'at the pool'.
2 personal name; from **Paul**.

Pollard
English – nickname; from Middle English meaning 'head', referring to someone with a large or misshapen head.

Pollitt

English – personal name; from a Middle English name **Ippollitts**, itself from a Greek name **Hippolytus** meaning 'letting loose the horses'.

Pollock

Other form: **Pollok**

Scottish – place name; from lands near Glasgow, the name probably deriving from Old Welsh meaning 'pool, pit'.

Polson

Other form: **Poulson**

English – personal name; from **Paul**, meaning 'son of **Paul**'.

Pomfret

Other forms: **Pontefract**

English – place name; from Pontefract in Yorkshire, the name deriving from Old French meaning 'broken bridge'.

Pomphrey

Other form: **Pumphrey**

Welsh – personal name; from Welsh 'ap' meaning 'son of' + **Humphrey**, itself Norman-French of Germanic origin meaning 'warrior' + 'peace'.

Pontefract other form of **Pomfret**

Popplewell

English – place name; from a place in Yorkshire, the name deriving from Old English meaning 'pebble' + 'spring, stream'.

Porteous

Scottish – Of obscure origin, possibly connected with Scots 'port' meaning 'gate'. John Porteous, Captain of the City Guard of Edinburgh, was lynched by the city mob in 1736, in what became known as the Porteous Riots.

Porter

English – occupational; from Middle English meaning 'door', referring to the occupation of door or gatekeeper, or from Old French meaning 'carrier of goods'.

Posnet, **Posnett**, **Posnette** other forms of **Postlethwaite**

Posselwhite other form of **Postlethwaite**

Postlethwaite

Other forms: **Posselwhite**, **Posnet(t)(e)**

English – place name; from Middle English meaning 'apostle' + northern Middle English meaning 'clearing'.

Potter

English – occupational; from Old English meaning 'potter'. Dennis Potter (1935–1996) was an English dramatist.

Potts

English

1 personal name; from **Philpot**, itself a double diminutive of the first name **Philip**.

2 occupational; from Old English meaning 'potter'.

Poulson other form of **Polson**

Poulton

English – place name; from many places, the name deriving from Old English meaning 'pool' + 'settlement'.

Powell

Other forms: **Bowell**, **Powles**

1 Welsh – personal name; from Welsh 'ap' meaning 'son of' + the Welsh name **Hywel**, itself from Welsh meaning 'eminent'.

2 English – personal name; other form of **Paul**.

Power

1 English and Irish – place name; from Pois in France, the name deriving from Old French meaning 'fish'.

2 English – nickname; from Middle English meaning 'poor', referring to someone poor, or a miser who claimed to be so.

Powles other form of **Powell**

Pratt

English – nickname; from Old English meaning 'trick', referring to a trickster or cunning person.

Preece other form of **Price**

Prendergast

Welsh – place name; from a place in Pembrokeshire, the origin of the name probably deriving from Old Welsh meaning 'castle' + 'village'.

Prentice

English – occupational/nickname; from Middle English meaning 'apprentice', referring either to a person learning a craft, or to someone jokingly referred to as a learner.

Prescott
English – place name; from places in the North West, Oxford and Shropshire, the name deriving from Old English meaning 'priest' + 'cottage'.

Presley other form of **Priestley**

Prewett
English – nickname; from Old French meaning 'valiant'.

Price
Other forms: **Pryce**, **Preece**
1 Welsh – personal name; from Welsh 'ap' meaning 'son of' + the name **Rhys**, itself from Welsh meaning 'ardour'.
2 English – occupational; from Middle English meaning 'price', referring to someone who fixed prices.

Prickett
English – nickname; from Middle English meaning 'a buck stag in its second year'.

Priddy
English – place name; from a place in Somerset, the name deriving from Old Welsh meaning 'earth house'.

Priestley
Other forms: **Presley**, **Prisley**
English – place name; from many places, the name deriving from Old English meaning 'priest' + 'wood, clearing'. Elvis Aaron Presley (1935–77) was an American pop singer.

Primrose
Scottish – place name; from places in Fife and Berwickshire, the name deriving from Old Welsh meaning 'tree' + 'moor'. It is the family name of the Earls of Rosebery.

Pringle
Scottish and N English – place name; from the lands of Hopringle in Midlothian, the name deriving from Old English meaning 'valley' + an Old Norse personal name (meaning 'pin, peg' + 'ravine').

Prisley other form of **Priestley**

Pritchard
Welsh – personal name; from Welsh 'ap' meaning 'son of' + **Richard**, itself from Norman-French of Germanic origin meaning 'strong' + 'ruler'.

Probert
Welsh – personal name; from Welsh 'ap' meaning 'son of' + **Robert**, itself from Old English meaning 'fame' + 'bright'.

Prosser
Welsh – personal name; from Welsh 'ap' meaning 'son of' + **Rosser**, itself of uncertain origin, possibly a Welsh form of **Roger.**

Protheroe
Other form: **Prydderch**
Welsh – personal name; from Welsh 'ap' meaning 'son of' + the name **Rhydderch**, itself from Welsh meaning 'reddish-brown' or 'famous'.

Provan
Scottish – place name; from the lands to the east of Glasgow, the name deriving from Middle English 'prebend' meaning 'lands providing revenue for the clergy'.

Pryce other form of **Price**

Prydderch other form of **Protheroe**

Puddephat
English – nickname; from Middle English meaning 'fat, barrel-shaped'.

Pugh
Welsh – personal name; from Welsh 'ap' meaning 'son of' + **Hugh.**

Pullen
English – occupational; from Old French meaning 'keeper of young horses'.

Pumphrey other form of **Pomphrey**

Purcell
Other form: **Pursell**
English – occupational; from Old French meaning 'piglet', referring to a keeper of pigs. See also **MacSporran**.

Purdy other form of **Pardoe**

Purkins other form of **Parkin**

Pursell other form of **Purcell.** See also **MacSporran**

Purves
Other form: **Purvis**
Scottish and English – occupational; probably from Middle English meaning 'provisions', referring to the person responsible for the supplies of a monastery or large household.

Pusey
Other forms: **Peasey**, **Pewsey**, **Pizzey**, **Pizzie**
English – place name; from Pusey in Berkshire, the name deriving from Old English meaning 'peas' + 'island'.

Putnam
Other form: **Puttenham**
English – place name; from places in Hertfordshire and Surrey, the name deriving from Old English meaning 'kite' + 'homestead'.

Pye
English – nickname; from Middle English meaning 'magpie', referring to a thief or a talkative person.

Pyke other form of **Pike**

Pymm
Other form: **Pim**
English – personal name; of uncertain origin, possibly from an Old English name **Pymma**.

Q

Quail, **Quaile** other forms of **Quayle**

Quainton
English – place name; from a place in Buckinghamshire, the name deriving from Old English meaning 'queen' + 'settlement'.

Quant
English – nickname; from Old French meaning 'cunning, smart'. Mary Quant (1934–) is a fashion and textile designer and a producer of cosmetics.

Quarendon
English – place name; from a place in Buckinghamshire, the name deriving from Old English meaning 'quern, millstone' + 'hill'.

Quartermain
Other form: **Quarterman**
English – nickname; from Old French meaning 'four hands', referring to a knight with mailed gauntlets, hence four hands.

Quayle
Other forms: **Quail**, **Quaile**
1 Manx – personal name; from Manx Gaelic meaning 'son of **Paul**'.
2 English – nickname; from Old French meaning 'quail', referring to someone with the bird's shyness.

Quenell other form of **Quennell**

Quennell
Other form: **Quenell**
English – personal name; from Old English meaning 'queen, woman' + 'war'.

Quested
English – place name; probably from Wherstead in Suffolk, the name deriving from Old English meaning 'wharfe' + 'place'.

Quick other form of **Quicke**

Quicke
Other form: **Quick**
English
1 nickname; from Old English meaning 'lively'.
2 place name; from places in Lancashire and Yorkshire, the name deriving from Old English meaning 'quickset hedge' or 'couch grass'; in the case of the name deriving from Cowick, it derives from Old English meaning 'cow' + farm'.

Quigley
Irish – personal name; anglicized form of Irish Gaelic **Ó Coigligh**, descendant of **Coigleach**, itself of uncertain meaning, possibly 'untidy'.

Quin
Other form: **Quinn**
Irish – personal name; anglicized form of Irish Gaelic **Ó Cuinn**, descendant of **Conn**, itself meaning 'counsel, sense'.

Quincey
Other form: **Quincy**
English – place name; from many places in France, the name deriving from a Latin name **Quintus**, itself meaning 'fifth'.

Quinn other form of **Quin**

Quinton
English
1 place name; from places in Gloucestershire, Northamptonshire and Worcestershire, the name deriving from Old English meaning 'queen' + 'settlement'.
2 personal name; from the first name **Quentin**, itself from Latin meaning 'fifth'.

Quirk
Irish and Manx – personal name; anglicized form of Irish Gaelic **Ó Cuirc**, descendant of **Corc**, itself meaning 'heart'.

R

Rabb other form of **Robert**

Rabson other form of **Robert**

Radcliffe other form of **Redcliffe**

Radley
English – place name; from places in Berkshire and Devonshire, the name deriving from Old English meaning 'red' + 'clearing'.

Rae
Scottish – nickname/place name; of doubtful origin, it may be from a lost place name or, more probably, a nickname from Older Scots meaning 'roe-deer'. The name originates in S and Central Scotland. See also **Ray** and **Roe.**

Raeburn
Scottish – place name; from a place in S Scotland, the name deriving from Older Scots meaning 'roe-deer' + stream'. Sir Henry Raeburn (1756–1823) was a distinguished Scottish portrait painter.

Rafe other form of **Ralph**

Raff other form of **Ralph**

Rafferty
Irish – personal name; anglicized form of Irish Gaelic **Ó Rabhartaigh**, descendant of **Robhartach**, itself meaning 'wielder of prosperity'.

Rainbow
Other form: **Raybould**
English – personal name; from Germanic meaning 'power' + 'bold', spelt thus because of a mistaken association with rainbows.

Rainey other form of **Rennie**

Raistrick other form of **Rastrick**

Rait
Other form: **Raitt**
Scottish – place name; from various places of this name, for example a ruined castle near Nairn, a village in Perthshire. The name derives from Scottish Gaelic meaning 'fort'.

Raleigh

English – place name; from a place in Devon, the name deriving from Old English meaning either 'red' or 'roe deer' + 'clearing'. Sir Walter Raleigh (1552–1618) was an English courtier, navigator and poet.

Ralfe other form of Ralph

Ralling, Rallison other forms of Rawlings

Ralls other form of Ralph

Ralph

Other forms: **Rafe**, **Raff**, **Ralfe**, **Ralls**, **Ralphson**, **Rawle**

English – personal name; from Norman-French of Germanic origin meaning 'counsel' + 'wolf'.

Ralston

Scottish – place name; from the lands near Paisley, the name deriving from Old English meaning 'Ralph's settlement'.

Ramage

Scottish – nickname; from Scots meaning 'wild, unruly'.

Rampton

English – place name; from places in Cambridgeshire and Nottinghamshire, the name deriving from Old English meaning 'ram' + 'settlement'.

Ramsay

Other form: **Ramsey**

Scottish and English – place name; from a place in Huntingdonshire, the name deriving from Old English meaning 'wild garlic' + 'island'. Allan Ramsay (1685–1758) was a Scottish poet; his more famous son of the same name (1713–84) was a portrait painter.

Ramsbotham

English – place name; from a place in Lancashire, the name deriving from Old English meaning 'wild garlic' + 'valley'.

Ramsey other form of Ramsay

Randall

Other forms: **Randle(s)**, **Rendell**

English – personal name; from a familiar form of the Middle English name **Rand**, itself from Germanic meaning 'shield'.

Randolph

English – personal name; from Old English meaning 'shield' + 'wolf'.

Rankin

Other form: **Rankine**

Scottish, N English, N Irish

1 personal name; from a familiar form of names beginning Ran- (such as **Randolph**).

2 personal name; in the Highlands, probably from Scottish Gaelic meaning 'son of the Frenchman'.

Rannie other form of **Rennie**

Ransley other form of **Rawnsley.**

Ransome

Other form: **Ransom, Ranson**

English – personal name; from **Rand** + 'son'. See **Randall.**

Rapson other form of **Robert**

Rastrick

Other form: **Raistrick**

English – place name; from a place in Yorkshire, the name deriving from Old Norse meaning either 'stream, ditch' + 'resting place' or 'plank bridge'.

Ratcliff other form of **Redcliffe**

Rathbone

Other form: **Rathborne**

English – place name; from places in Warwickshire and Derbyshire, the name deriving from Old English meaning 'reeds' + 'stream'.

Rattray

Scottish – place name; from the place in Perthshire, the name probably deriving from Old Welsh meaning 'fort' + 'settlement'.

Rawle other form of **Ralph**

Rawlings

Other forms: **Rawlins, Ralling, Rallison**

English – personal name; from a short form of **Raw**, a medieval name which is another form of **Ralph**, itself from Norman-French of Germanic origin meaning 'counsel' + 'wolf'.

Rawnsley

Other form: **Ransley**

English – place name; from a place in Yorkshire, the name deriving from Old English meaning 'raven' + 'hill'.

Ray
Other forms: **Fitzroy, Rey, Roy**
English
1 nickname; from Old French meaning 'king', referring to someone who played the part of a king in a pageant, or to someone with a regal manner.
2 nickname; other form of **Rae**.
3 place name; from Middle English meaning 'at the island', or 'at the river'.
4 place name; other form of **Wray.**

Raybould other form of **Rainbow**

Raymond
Other form: **Raymont, Redmond** (Irish)
English and Irish – personal name; from Norman-French of Germanic origin meaning 'counsel' + 'protection'.

Rayner
English – personal name; from Norman-French of Germanic origin meaning 'might' + 'army'.

Read
Other forms: **Reade, Reed, Reid**
English
1 nickname; from Old English meaning 'red', referring to a red-haired or red-complexioned person.
2 place name; from many places, the name deriving from Old English meaning 'rough place, clearing' or 'roe headland'.

Reagan other form of **Regan**

Realy, Really other form of **Reilly**

Reckett other form of **Rich**

Redcliffe
Other forms: **Radcliffe, Ratcliff**
English – place name; from many places, the name deriving from Old English meaning 'red' + 'cliff'.

Redfern
English – place name; from a place near Rochdale, the name deriving from Old English meaning 'red' + 'fern, bracken'.

Redgrave
English – place name; from a place in Suffolk, the name deriving from Old English meaning 'reed' + 'ditch'.

Redmond Irish form of **Raymond**

Redpath
Scottish – place name; from the village in Berwickshire, the name probably of obvious derivation. Anne Redpath (1895–1965) was a well-known painter, and Jean Redpath (1937–) is a folk singer.

Reece other form of **Rhys**

Reed other form of **Read**

Rees other form of **Rhys**

Reeve
English – occupational; from Middle English meaning 'steward, bailiff'.

Regan
Other forms: **Reagan**, **O Regan**
Irish – personal name; anglicized form of Irish Gaelic **Ó Ríagáin**, descendant of **Riagán**, itself perhaps meaning 'impulsive, furious'. Ronald Wilson Reagan (1911–) was 40th president of the USA.

Reid Scottish form of **Read**

Reilly
Other forms: **Real(l)y**, **Riley**
Irish – personal name; from an Irish Gaelic personal name **Raghailleach**, itself of unknown origin.

Reith
Scottish – personal name; of doubtful origin; it may be derived from **MacReath** (itself a variant of **MacRae**). Lord Reith (John Reith) (1889–1971) was the controversial first Director-General of the BBC.

Renaud other form of **Reynold**

Rendell other form of **Randall**

Rennard other form of **Reynard**

Rennie
Other forms: **Renny**, **Rainey**, **Rannie**
Scottish and N Irish (mainly **Rainey**)
personal name; familiar form of first names such as **Reynold.**

Renton
N English and Scottish – place name; from a place in Berwickshire, the name deriving from an Old English name meaning 'power' + 'settlement'.

Rey other form of **Ray**

Reynard
Other form: **Rennard**
English – personal name; from Norman-French of Germanic origin meaning 'counsel' + 'brave'.

Reynell other form of **Reynold**

Reynold
Other forms: **Reynoldson, Renaud, Reynell**
English – personal name; from a Germanic name meaning 'counsel' + 'rule'.

Rhodes
Other forms: **Roads, Royd, Rodd**
English – place name; from Old English meaning 'woodland clearing'.

Rhys
Other forms: **Reece, Rees, Rice**
Welsh – personal name; from an Old Welsh name **Ris,** itself meaning 'fiery warrior'.

Rian other form of **Ryan**

Riccard other form of **Richard**

Rice other form of **Rhys**

Rich
Other forms: **Reckett, Rickett, Ricks, Ritch, Ritchie, Rixon**
English
1 nickname; from Middle English meaning 'wealthy', referring to a rich man, or, ironically, to a very poor one.
2 personal name; from a short form of **Richard.**
3 place name; from a lost place in Leicestershire, the name deriving from Old English meaning 'drainage channel'.

Richard
Other forms: **Pritchard** (Welsh), **Riccard, Richards, Richardson, Ritchard, Rickard, Ritson**
English – personal name; from Germanic meaning 'strong' + 'ruler'.

Rickett other form of **Rich**

Ricks other form of **Rich**

Riddell
Other forms: **Riddel, Riddle**
[in Scotland usually pronounced 'riddle']
Scottish and N English
1 place name; from Ryedale in N Yorkshire, itself from an Old Welsh river name + 'valley'.
2 personal name; from a Norman-French name, possibly deriving from Germanic meaning 'ride'.

Rideout
English – nickname; from 'ride out', probably referring to a rider.

Ridgeway
English – place name; from numerous places, the name deriving from Old English meaning 'ridge' + 'road'.

Ridley
English – place name; from places in Northumberland and Cheshire, the name deriving from Old English meaning 'cleared, cut down' + 'wood, clearing'.

Rigby
English – place name; meaning 'ridge' + 'farm'.

Riley other form of **Reilly**

Rimer
Other form: **Rimmer**
English – occupational; from Middle English meaning 'to compose or recite verse', referring to a poet or minstrel.

Ritch other form of **Rich**

Ritchard other form of **Richard**

Ritchie
Scottish and English – personal name; from a familiar form of **Richard**; also found as **MacRitchie** in N Scotland.

Ritson other form of **Richard**

Rixon other form of **Rich**

Roach
Other forms: **Roche, Rockall**
English – place name; from Middle English meaning 'crag' or 'rocky outcrop'.

Roads other form of **Rhodes**

Robart other form of **Robert**

Robb, Robbins other forms of **Robert**

Robert
Other forms: **Rabb, Rabson, Rapson, Robart, Robb, Robbins, Roberts, Robertson, Robinson, Rob(e)son, Roblin, Roby**
English – personal name; from Old English meaning 'fame' + 'bright'. Heath Robinson (1872–1944) was an English humorist and cartoonist.

Roche other form of **Roach**

Rockall other form of **Roach**

Rodd other form of **Rhodes**

Rodger, Rodgers other forms of **Roger**

Rodgett other form of **Roger**

Roe
English – nickname; from Old English meaning 'roe deer', referring to a fast runner

Roff other form of **Rolfe**

Roger
Other forms: **Rodger(s), Rogers, Rogger; Rosser** and **Prosser** (both Welsh), **Rodgett, Rudge, Rogerson**
1 English – personal name; from Norman-French of Germanic origin meaning 'fame' + 'spear'.
2 Irish – personal name; anglicized form of Irish Gaelic **Mac Ruaidhrí**, itself from Celtic meaning 'red' + 'rule'.

Rolance other form of **Rowland**

Roland, Rolland other forms of **Rowland**

Rolfe
Other forms: **Roff, Rolph, Ruff, Ruffell**
English – personal name; from a medieval name **Rolf**, itself from Germanic meaning 'fame' + 'wolf'.

Roll other form of **Rollo**

Rollins other form of **Rollo**

Rollison other form of **Rollo**

Rollo
Other forms: **Roll, Rollins, Rollison, Rolls, Rowles, Rowlinson**
English – personal name; from **Roul** which is the Norman form of

Rolf (see **Rolfe**). Charles Stewart Rolls (1877–1910) was an English car manufacturer and aviator who was a partner of Henry Royce.

Rolph other form of **Rolfe**

Ronson other form of **Rowland**

Rose
Other forms: **Royce**, **Royse**, **Ruskin**
English – personal name; from a Middle English personal name, itself from Norman-French of Germanic origin meaning 'fame' + 'kind'. Sir Frederick Henry Royce (1863–1933) founded Rolls Royce, manufacturers of cars and aero engines together with Charles Rolls.

Ross
Other form: **Rosse**
place name;
1 English and Scottish – From Rots in Normandy, itself probably from Germanic meaning 'clearing'.
2 Scottish and English – From various places, the name deriving from a Celtic word meaning 'headland', as in the former county of Ross and Cromarty.

Rosser
Other form: **Prosser**
Welsh – personal name; of unknown origin, possibly a Welsh form of **Roger.**

Rothwell
English – place name; from places in Lincolnshire, Northamptonshire and Yorkshire, the name deriving from Old English meaning 'clearing' + 'spring'.

Rouse other form of **Rowse**

Rousel other form of **Russell**

Rowbotham other form of **Rowbottom**

Rowbottom
Other form: **Rowbotham**
English – place name; from Old English meaning 'rough' + 'valley'.

Rowe
English
1 place name; from Old English meaning 'row' (of houses).
2 nickname; from Old English meaning 'rough'.

Rowland
Other forms: **Rol(l)and**, **Ronson**, **Rowlandson**, **Rolance**
English – personal name; from a Norman name **Rolant**, itself from Germanic meaning 'fame' + 'territory'.

Rowles other form of **Rollo**

Rowley
English – place name; from several places, the name deriving from Old English meaning 'rough wood' + 'clearing'.

Rowlinson other form of **Rollo**

Rowntree
English – place name; from Middle English meaning 'mountain ash, rowan' + 'tree'. Joseph Rowntree (1836–1925) was an English Quaker industrialist, cocoa manufacturer and reformer.

Rowse
Other forms: **Rouse**, **Russ**
English – nickname; from Middle English meaning 'red-haired'.

Rowsell other form of **Russell**

Roy other form of **Ray**

Royal other form of **Royle**

Royce other form of **Rose**

Royd other form of **Rhodes**

Roylance other form of **Rylands**

Royle
Other forms: **Royal**, **Ryle**
English – place name; from Old English meaning 'roe deer' + 'hill'.

Royse other form of **Rose**

Ruddick
Other form: **Ruddock**
English – nickname; from Old English meaning 'robin redbreast'.

Rudge
Other form: **Ruggles**
English
1 place name; from a place in Shropshire, the name deriving from Middle English meaning 'ridge'
2 personal name; from a medieval familiar form of **Roger.**
3 nickname; from Old French meaning 'red', for a red-haired person.

Ruff other form of **Rolfe**

Ruffell other form of **Rolfe**

Ruggles other form of **Rudge**

Rumbelow
English – place name; from several places, the name deriving from Old English meaning 'at the three hills or tumuli'.

Rumble other form of **Rumbold.**

Rumbold
Other forms: **Rumble, Rumpole**
English – personal name; from a Norman-French name **Rumbald**, itself from Germanic meaning 'renown' + 'bold'.

Runcie other form of **Runciman**

Runciman
Other form: **Runcie**
English – occupational; from Old French meaning 'nag' + 'man', referring to someone who looked after the nags.

Ruskin
English – personal name; probably from a familiar form of **Rose.**

Russ other form of **Rowse**

Russell
Other forms: **Rowsell, Rousel**
English, Irish and Scottish – nickname; from a nickname **Rousel**, itself from Norman-French of Germanic origin referring to someone with red hair.

Rutherford
Scottish – place name; from the lands in Roxburghshire, the name deriving from Old English meaning 'cattle' + 'ford'. Ernest Rutherford (1871–1937) was a New Zealand-born physicist who was a pioneer of subatomic physics.

Rutter
English
1 occupational; from Middle English meaning 'rote', referring to a player of the rote, a medieval stringed instrument,
2 nickname; from Old French meaning 'highwayman, robber', referring to a dishonest person, or a criminal.

Ryan
Other forms: **O Ryan**, **Rian**

Irish – personal name; anglicized form of Irish Gaelic **Ó Riain**, descendant of **Rian** or **Riaghan**, itself possibly meaning 'great, big' + 'splendid'.

Rylance other form of **Ryland**

Ryland
Other form: **Roylance**, **Rylance**, **Rylands**

English – place name; from Old English meaning 'rye' + 'land'.

Ryle other form of **Royle**

S

Sacker
Other form: **Secker**
English – occupational; from Old English meaning 'sackcloth maker'.

Sainsbury
Other form: **Saintsbury**
English – place name; from a place in Gloucestershire, the name deriving from an Old English personal name meaning 'male' + 'friend' + 'fortress'.

Saint
Other form: **Sant**
English – nickname; from Old French meaning 'saint', referrring to someone extremely devout.

Sainter
Other form: **Santer**
English – nickname; from Old French meaning 'without' + 'land', referring to someone who had inherited no land.

Saintsbury other form of **Sainsbury**

Salaman other form of **Salamon**

Salamon
Other forms: **Salaman, Salmon**
English – personal name; from the medieval form of **Solomon**, itself from Hebrew meaning 'peace'.

Salinger
English – place name; from Saint-Léger in France. J D Salinger (1919–) is an American novelist and short story writer.

Salisberry other form of **Salisbury**

Salisbury
Other form: **Salisberry**
English – place name; probably from a place in Lancashire, the name deriving from Old English meaning 'willow pool' + 'fortress'. It is also possible that it derives from the city of Salisbury in Wiltshire, the name in this case deriving from Old English meaning 'armour' + 'fortress'

Salmon other form of **Salaman**

Sambrook
Other form: **Sandbrook**
English – place name; from a place in Shropshire, the name deriving from Old English meaning 'sand' + 'stream'.

Samm, Samms other forms of **Samuel**

Sampson other form of **Samson**

Samson
Other forms: **Sampson, Sankin, Sansam, Sansome**
English – personal name; from Hebrew, probably meaning 'sun'.

Samuel
Other forms: **Samm(s), Samwell**
English – personal name; from Hebrew, probably meaning 'requested of God'.

Sandbrook other form of **Sambrook**

Sanders, Sanderson other forms of **Alexander**

Sanger other form of **Sangster**

Sangster
Other form: **Sanger**
English – occupational; from Old English meaning 'singer, chorister'.

Sankin other form of **Samson**

Sansam other form of **Samson**

Sansome other form of **Samson**

Sant other form of **Saint**

Santer other form of **Sainter**

Saunders other form of **Alexander**

Sawbridge
English – place name; from a place in Warwickshire, the name deriving from Old English meaning 'willows' + 'bridge'.

Sawyer
Other form: **Sayer**
English – occupational; from Middle English meaning 'to saw', referring to someone who sawed wood. See also **Sayers.**

Sayer other form of **Sawyer** or **Sayers**

Sayers
Other forms: **Sayer, Seers, Seyers**
1 English – personal name; either from a Middle English name **Saher** or **Seir** from Germanic meaning 'victory' + 'army' or else from an Old English name **Saehere** meaning 'sea' + 'army'.
2 English – occupational; from Middle English meaning 'sawer' referring to a woodcutter (see also **Sawyer**), or else from Middle English meaning 'to say', referring to a professional reciter of verse, or from Middle English meaning 'to test', referring to an assayer of metals.
3 Welsh – occupational; from Welsh meaning 'carpenter, wright'.

Scales
Other form: **Scholes**
English – place name; from places in Cumbria and Lancashire, the name deriving from Old Norse meaning 'huts'.

Scarfe
English – nickname; from Old Norse meaning 'cormorant'.

Scargill
English – place name; from a place in Yorkshire, the name deriving from Old Norse meaning 'diving duck' + 'ravine'. Arthur Scargill (1938–) is an English miner and trade union leader.

Schofield other form of **Scholfield**

Scholes other form of **Scales**

Scholfield
Other form: **Schofield**
English – place name; from Old English meaning 'hut' + 'field'.

Scott
Scottish and N English – nickname; referring to someone from Scotland or to a Gaelic-speaking Highlander. Sir Walter Scott (1771–1832) was a Scottish novelist.

Scudamore other form of **Skidmore**

Searle
English – personal name; from a Norman-French name **Serlo**, itself probably from Germanic meaning 'defender'.

Seaton
Other form: **Seton**
1 English and Scottish – place name; from various places of this name, deriving from Old English meaning 'sea' +'settlement'.

2 Scottish – place name; from the place in E Lothian, the name deriving from Sai in Normandy + Old English meaning 'settlement'.

Secker other form of **Sacker**

Sedgewick
Other forms: **Sidgwick**, **Sidgewick**
English – place name; from a place in Cumbria, the name deriving from a Middle English personal name **Sigge**, itself from Old English meaning 'victory' + 'outlying dairy farm'.

Seers other form of **Sayers**

Sefton
Other form: **Sephton**
English – place name; from a place in Lancashire, the name deriving from Old Norse meaning 'rush' + Old English 'settlement'.

Sellar, **Sellars** other forms of **Seller**

Seller
Other forms: **Sellar(s)**, **Sellers**, **Sell(s)**
English
1 place name/occupational; from Middle English meaning 'hut', referring either to a place with such a building on it, or to the job of herdsman and the dwelling associated with it.
2 occupational; from Old French meaning 'saddle', referring to a saddler.
3 occupational; from Old French meaning 'small room, cellar', referring to someone who worked in the cellars or stores of a house or monastery.
4 occupational; from Middle English meaning 'to sell', referrring to a trader or merchant. Peter Sellers (1925–80) was an English actor.

Semkin other form of **Simkin**

Semper
Other form: **Simper**
English – place name; from various places in France called St Pierre after St Peter.

Sempill other form of **Semple**

Semple
Other form: **Sempill**
1 Scottish, English and N Irish – place name; from various place in Normandy called Saint-Paul or Saint-Pol.
2 English and Scottish – nickname; from Old French meaning 'simple'.

Sephton other form of **Sefton**

Sessions
English – place name; from Soissons in France, the name deriving from the name of a Gaulish tribe.

Seton other form of **Seaton**

Sexton
English – occupational; from Old French meaning 'sacristan'.

Seyers other form of **Sayers**

Seymour
English
1 place name; from a place in France, the name deriving from the name of the church dedicated to St Maur.
2 place name; from a place in Yorkshire, the name deriving from Old English meaning 'sea' + 'lake'.

Shackleton
English – place name; from a place in Yorkshire, the name deriving from Old English meaning 'tongue of land' + 'settlement'.

Shaddock other form of **Chadwick**

Shadwell
English – place name; from many places, the name deriving from Old English meaning 'boundary' + 'stream', though in some cases it may derive from Old English meaning 'shady' + 'stream'.

Shakeshaft
English – nickname; from Old English meaning 'to brandish' + 'lance, spear'.

Shakespeare
English – nickname; from Middle English meaning 'to brandish' + 'spear', referring to an aggressive or rowdy person. William Shakespeare (1564–1616) English playwright, poet, actor-manager, was the most famous bearer of this name.

Shanks
English – nickname; from Old English meaning 'legs', referring to someone with conspicuous legs or a fast running speed.

Shannon
Irish – place name; from the River Shannon in Ireland.

Sharman other form of **Sherman**

Shaw
Other form: **Shay**
1 English and Scottish – place name; from Old English meaning 'thicket', from one of the many places of this name.
2 Scottish – personal name; from one of several Gaelic names meaning 'wolf'.
3 English – nickname; from Middle English meaning 'to spoil, to waste', referring to a destructive person.

Shearer
Scottish and N English – occupational; meaning either a person who clipped the surface of cloth, or a sheep-shearer. Compare **Sherman**.

Shearman other form of **Sherman**

Sheen
English – place name; from places in Surrey and Staffordshire, the name deriving from Old English meaning 'sheds, huts'.

Shelley
English – place name; from many places, the name deriving from Old English meaning 'shelf, cliff' + 'wood' or 'clearing'. Percy Bysshe Shelley (1792–1822) was an English poet.

Shelton
Other form: **Shilton**
place name; the name deriving from Old English meaning 'shelf, cliff' + 'settlement'.

Sherlock
Other form: **Shurlock**
English – nickname; from Old English meaning 'bright' + 'lock of hair', referring to a fair or blond person.

Sherman
Other forms: **Sharman**, **Shearman**
English – occupational; from Old English meaning 'cutter, shear man', referring to someone in the woollen trade who cut the nap from the cloth. Compare **Shearer**.

Sherwin
English – nickname; from Middle English meaning 'to shear' + 'wind', referring to a fast runner.

Shields
English – place name; from places in Northumberland and Durham,

the name deriving from Old English meaning either 'at the shed' or 'at the shallows'.

Shilton other form of **Shelton**

Shipton
English – place name; from many places, the name deriving from Old English meaning 'sheep' + 'enclosure'.

Shuck other form of **Shuker**

Shufflebotham
English – place name; from a place in Lancashire, the name deriving from Old English meaning 'spring where sheep are washed' + 'valley'.

Shuker
Other form: **Shuck**
English – nickname; from Old English meaning 'devil, goblin'.

Shurlock other form of **Sherlock**

Shutt
English – occupational; from Middle English meaning 'shoot', referring to an archer.

Shuttleworth
English – place name; from places in Derbyshire, Lancashire and Yorkshire, the name deriving from Old English meaning 'bolt, bar' + 'enclosure', that is a place enclosed by a bolted gate.

Siddall
English – place name; from places in Lancashire, the name deriving from Old English meaning 'wide' + 'nook, recess'.

Sidgwick, Sidgewick other forms of **Sedgewick**

Sidney
Other form: **Sydney**
English – place name; either from places in Surrey and Lincolnshire, the name deriving from Old English meaning 'wide' + 'island', or from a place in Normandy, after a church dedicated to St Denis.

Silcock, Sill other forms of **Silvester**

Silvester
Other forms: **Silcock, Sill**
English – personal name; from the first name, itself from Latin meaning 'of the woods'

Sim

Other forms: **Simcock, Simcox, Simpson, Simson, Syme**

English – personal name; from a medieval name **Sim**, itself a short form of **Simon.**

Simeon other form of **Simon**

Simkin

Other forms: **Semkin, Simpkin, Simpkinson, Sinkin, Sinkinson**

English – personal name; from a medieval name, itself a diminutive of **Sim.**

Simmonds, Simmons other forms of **Simon**

Simon

Other forms: Simeon, Symon, **Symonds, Simmon(d)s, Syson, Fitzsimmons**

English – personal name; from the English form of the Hebrew name **Simeon**, itself from Hebrew meaning 'listening'.

Simper other form of **Semper**

Simpkin other form of **Simkin**

Simpkinson other form of **Simkin**

Simpson other form of **Sim**

Simson other form of **Sim**

Sinclair

Scottish and English – [in Scotland usually pronounced 'sinkler'] place name; from one of two places in Normandy called Saint-Clair. It is the family name of the Earls of Caithness.

Singleton

English – place name; from places in Sussex and Lancashire, the name in the first case deriving from Old English meaning 'burnt clearing' + 'settlement', the second from Old English meaning 'shingle' (roof or building)' + 'settlement'.

Sinkin, Sinkinson other forms of **Simkin**

Sinnett other form of **Sinnott**

Sinnott

Other forms: **Sinnett, Synott**

English – personal name; from an Old English name **Sigenoth**, itself meaning 'victory' + 'bold'.

Sisley

Other form: **Sisson**

English – personal name; from the medieval name **Sisley** or **Cecilie**, itself from Latin meaning 'blind'.

Sixsmith

English – occupational; from Old English meaning 'scythe maker'.

Skeate

English – nickname; from Old Norse meaning 'swift'.

Skeffington

Other form: **Skivington**

English – place name; from a place in Leicestershire, the name deriving from an Old English name + 'tribe' + 'settlement'.

Skelton

English – place name; from many places, the name deriving from Old English meaning 'bank, hill' + 'settlement'.

Skidmore

Other form: **Scudamore**

English – place name; from Old English meaning 'mud' + 'moor'.

Skinner

English – occupational; from Middle English meaning 'hide, pelt', referrring to a stripper of furs or hides in the tanning industry.

Skivington other form of **Skeffington**

Slack

English – place name; from Old Norse meaning 'shallow valley'.

Slade

English – place name; from places in Devon and Somerset, the name deriving from Old English meaning 'small valley'.

Sloan

Other form: **Sloane**

Irish and Scottish – personal name; from a Gaelic name **Sluaghadan**, itself meaning 'raid'.

Slocombe

Other form: **Slocum**

English – place name; from places in the Isle of Wight and Devon, the name deriving from Old English meaning 'sloe' + 'valley'.

Smeaton

Other form: **Smeeton**

English and Scottish – place name; from places in Cornwall, Yorkshire and near Edinburgh, the name deriving from Old English meaning 'smiths' + 'settlement'.

Smedley

English – place name; from a place in Lancashire, the name deriving from Old English meaning 'smooth, level' + 'clearing'.

Smee

English – place name; from Old English meaning 'smooth, level'.

Smeeton other form of **Smeaton**

Smith

Other form: **Smithers**, **Smithson**, **Smythe**

English – occupational; from Middle English meaning 'smith', referring to a worker in metal, one of the most important crafts, giving rise to one of the most common surnames.

Smollet

English and Scottish – nickname; from Old English meaning 'small head'. Tobias Smollett (1721–71) was an 18th-century Scottish novelist.

Smythe other form of **Smith**

Snape

English – place name; from many places, the name deriving in the south from Old English meaning 'boggy patch', but in the north more likely to derive from Old Norse meaning 'poor grazing'.

Snell

Other forms: **Snelling**, **Snelson**

English – nickname; from Middle English meaning 'lively', referring to a quick, vivacious person.

Snowden

English – place name; from a place in Yorkshire, the name deriving from Old English meaning 'snow' + 'hill'.

Soames

English – place name; from Old English meaning 'lake' + 'homestead'.

Somerville
Other form: **Sommerville**
Scottish – place name; from a place in Normandy, itself from a
Germanic personal name **Sigimar** + Old French meaning 'settlement'.

Soper
English – occupational; from Middle English meaning 'soap',
referring to a maker of soap.

Sotheby
Other form: Sotherby
English – place name; from Old Norse meaning 'south' +'village'

Soutar
Other form: **Souter**
Scottish – occupational; from Scots meaning 'shoemaker'. William
Soutar (1898–1943) was a Scottish poet.

Sowden
English – nickname; from Middle English meaning 'sultan', referring
either to someone who played such a role in a pageant, or to an
arrogant, domineering person.

Spark
Other forms: **Spragg, Sprague, Sprake**
English – nickname; from Old Norse meaning 'bright, lively'. Muriel
Spark (1918–) is a Scottish writer.

Speight
English – nickname; from Middle English meaning 'woodpecker',
referring to an insistent chatterer.

Speir other form of **Speirs**

Speirs
Other forms: **Speir, Spier(s)**
Scottish and English
1 occupational; from Middle English meaning 'watchman'.
2 nickname; from Middle English meaning 'spear', probably referring
to a tall thin person.

Spence
Other forms: **Spencer, Spens, Spenser**
English – occupational; from Middle English meaning 'larder',
referring to someone working in the pantry of a house or monastery.
Lady Diana Frances Spencer (1961–) is the ex-wife of Charles, Prince
of Wales.

Spier, Spiers other forms of **Speir**

Spiller

English – occupational; from Middle English meaning 'to play', referring to a tumbler or jester.

Spode

English – place name; from a place in Shropshire, the name deriving from Old English meaning 'spade', probably referring to a spade-shaped field. Josiah Spode (1754–1827) was an English potter who produced fine porcelain.

Spong

English – place name; from a Middle English dialect word meaning 'long narrow strip of land'.

Spooner

English – occupational; from Middle English meaning 'person who covered roofs with shingle'. Later, the word came to be associated with the eating utensil and thus the name may in some cases refer to a maker of spoons. William A Spooner (1844–1930) was an Oxford don whose nervous habit of transposing letters or syllables became known as spoonerisms.

Spragge, Sprague, Sprake other forms of **Spark**

Squire

Other form: **Swire**

English – occupational; from Old French meaning 'shield bearer' and originally referring to a youth who attended on a knight, but later to a person below the rank of knight.

Stacey

English – personal name; from a short form of **Eustace**, itself from Greek meaning 'fruitful'.

Stack

English – occupational/nickname; from Old Norse meaning 'stack, pile', referring either to a person who stacked hay, or to a person as big as a haystack.

Stalker

Scottish and N English – occupational/nickname; meaning either a deerstalker or a nickname for a stealthy person.

Stallabrass other form of **Stallybrass**

Stallybrass
Other form: **Stallabrass**
English – place name; from a place in Essex, the name probably deriving from Middle English meaning 'strong, stalwart' + 'arm'.

Stamp
English – place name; from a place in France, the name deriving from an Old French place name Estampes, itself of uncertain origin.

Standley, **Stanleigh** other forms of **Stanley**

Stanley
Other forms: **Standley**, **Stanleigh**
English place name; from places in Derbyshire, Durham, and Gloucestershire, the name deriving from Old English meaning 'stone' + 'clearing'.

Stannard
English – personal name; from an Old English name **Stanheard**, itself meaning 'stone' + 'brave'.

Stapleton
English and Irish – place name; from many places, the name deriving from Old English meaning 'post' + 'settlement'.

Stark
Other forms: **Starkie**, **Starkey**
Scottish and N English – nickname; from Middle English meaning 'firm, strong', referring to a resolute, strong person.

Statham
English – place name; from a place in Cheshire, the name deriving from Old English meaning 'at the landing stages'.

Stenhouse
Scottish – place name; from a place near Falkirk, the name deriving from Scots meaning 'stone' + 'house'.

Stephen
Other forms: **Stephens**, **Stephenson**, **Steven(s)**, **Stevenson**
English – personal name; from the Middle English name **Stephen**, itself from Greek meaning 'crown'.

Steuart other form of **Stewart**.

Steven, **Stevens**, **Stevenson** other forms of **Stephen**.

Stewart

Other forms: **Stuart, Steuart**

Scottish – occupational; from the adminstrator of a household, especially a royal household, the name deriving from Old English meaning 'house' + 'guardian'. The royal house of Stewart descended from Walter, a 14th-century Steward of Scotland who married Marjorie, daughter of King Robert the Bruce. The form Stuart came from French (which has no 'w'), probably at the time of Mary, Queen of Scots in the 16th century. As well as a royal surname, it is widespread in Scotland and is a common name among travelling people.

Stirling

Scottish – place name; from the town on the River Forth; the name is of obscure origin.

Stopford

Other forms: **Stopforth, Stoppard**

English – place name; from Stockport in Cheshire, the name deriving from Old English meaning 'hamlet' + market'. Stoppard is the adopted surname of the Czech-born dramatist Thomas Straussler who settled in Britain in 1946.

Storey

English – personal name; from an Old Norse name **Stori**, itself meaning 'big'.

Stott

English and Scottish – nickname/occupational; from Middle English meaning 'bull, steer', the term also being used for a horse, a heifer or as a term of abuse for a woman. The name may also refer to someone who was a keeper of animals.

Stuart other form of **Stewart**

Stubbins, Stubbing other forms of **Stubbs**

Stubbs

Other forms: **Stubbing, Stubbins**

English – place name/nickname; from Old English meaning 'tree stumps', referring to a clearing, or else 'short, stumpy', referring to a squat figure.

Sugden

English – place name; from a place in Yorkshire, the name deriving from Old English meaning 'sparrow' + 'valley'.

Sullivan
Irish – personal name; anglicized form of Irish Gaelic **Ó Súileabháin**, descendant of **Súileabhán**, itself meaning 'eye' + 'black'.

Sumner
English – occupational; from Middle English meaning 'summoner', referring to a court official who was in charge of ensuring that witnesses appeared in court.

Sutcliffe
English – place name; from places in Yorkshire, the name deriving from Old English meaning 'south' + 'cliff'.

Swain
English – occupational; from Old Norse meaning 'servant, attendant'.

Swire other form of **Squire**

Sydney other form of **Sidney**

Sykes
English – place name; from Middle English meaning 'marshy stream,' or 'damp valley'.

Syme other form of **Sim**

Symon, Symonds other forms of **Simon**

Synott other form of **Sinnott**

Syson other form of **Simon**

T

Tague other form of **Tighe**

Tait

Scottish and N English – nickname; from Old Norse meaning 'cheerful'. Compare **Tate.**

Talbot

English – personal name; probably from a Germanic name meaning 'destroy' + 'message'.

Tammage other form of **Tollemache**

Tandy

English – personal name; from a familiar form of **Andrew**.

Tanner

English – occupational; from Middle English meaning 'tanner of animal skins'.

Tansley

English – place name; from a place in Derbyshire, the name deriving from Old English meaning 'branching valley' + 'clearing'.

Taplin other form of **Tapp**

Tapp

Other form: **Taplin**

English – personal name; from an Old English name **Taeppa**, itself of unknown meaning.

Tapper other form of **Tapster**

Tapster

Other form: **Tapper**

English – occupational; from Middle English meaning 'to draw off' (from a cask or barrel), referring to the occupation of a tavern keeper or wine merchant.

Tarbock

Other form: **Tarbuck**

English – place name; from a place in Lancashire, the name deriving from Old English meaning 'thorn bush' + 'brook'.

Tarleton
English – place name; from places in Lancashire and Gloucestershire, the name deriving from the Old Norse god **Thor** + 'ruler' + Old English meaning 'settlement'.

Tarrant
English – place name; from many places in Dorset and Hampshire, the name deriving from an Old Welsh river name of uncertain meaning.

Tarry other form of **Terry**

Tasker
English – occupational; from Old French meaning either 'piece worker' or 'task-master'.

Tatam other form of **Tatham**

Tate
English – personal name; from an Old English name **Tata**, itself of uncertain meaning. Compare **Tait.**

Tatham
Other forms: **Tatam**, **Tatum**
English – place name; from a place in Lancashire, the name deriving from an Old English name **Tata** + 'homestead'.

Tayler other form of **Taylor**

Taylor
Other forms: **Tayler**, **Taylour**
English – occupational; from Old French meaning 'cutter', referring to a tailor.

Tebbit, Tebboth other forms of **Tibb**

Teek other form of **Tighe**

Tegg
Other form: **Tigg**
1 Welsh – nickname; from Welsh meaning 'beautiful', referring to a handsome person.
2 English – occupational; from Middle English meaning 'sheep in its second year', referring to a shepherd.

Telfair, Telfer other forms of **Telford**

Telford
Other forms: **Telfair**, **Telfer**
Scottish and N English – nickname; from Old French meaning 'cut' + 'iron', referring to someone whose weapon could pierce his enemy's

armour. Thomas Telford (1757–1834) was a pioneering Scottish engineer.

Temple
Other form: **Templeman**
English
1 occupational; from Middle English meaning 'temple', a type of house kept by the Knights Templar, a crusading order named thus because they claimed to have occupied the site of the Temple in Jerusalem. The surname refers to those inhabiting and employed in such temples by the Knights Templar.
2 nickname; from Middle English meaning 'temple' (see above), referring to orphans and foundlings baptized at the Temple Church in London, the name of the church deriving from the fact that it was built on a site owned by the Knights Templar.

Tennant
Other form: **Tennent**
English and Scottish – occupational; from Middle English meaning 'landholder', referring to a farmer in the Middle Ages who held his land in return for service to an overlord.

Tenney
Other forms: **Tennison, Tennyson**
English – personal name; from a familiar form of **Dennis**, itself from **Dionysius**, the name of the Greek god of wine. Alfred, 1st Baron Tennyson (1809–92), was an English poet.

Terry
Other forms: **Tarry, Torry**
English – personal name; from **Therry**, itself from Norman-French of Germanic origin meaning 'people' + 'power'.

Thacker other form of **Thatcher**

Tharp other form of **Thorpe**

Thatcher
Other forms: **Thacker, Theaker**
English – occupational; from Old English and Old Norse meaning 'to cover', referring to the craft of roofing a thatched cottage. Margaret Hilda Thatcher (1925–) was the first woman party leader and prime minister in British politics.

Theobald
Other forms: **Dybell, Tippett, Tipple, Tudball**
English – personal name; from a medieval name **Tebald**, itself from
Germanic meaning 'people' + 'brave'. See also **Tibb**.

Thewles
Other forms: **Thewless, Thouless**
English – nickname; from Old English meaning 'muscle' + 'without',
referring to someone without good qualities.

Thin
Other form: **Thynne**
English – nickname; from Middle English meaning 'thin'.

Thirkell, Thirkle other forms of **Thurkettle**

Thom other form of **Thomas**

Thomas
Other forms: **Thom, Tomkin, Tomkiss, Tomlin, Tomlinson,
Tompkin, Thompson, Thomson, Tonkin, Tonks**
English – personal name; from Aramaic meaning 'twin'. Dylan
Thomas (1914–53) was a Welsh poet.

Thorburn
Scottish and N English – personal name; from either of two names
deriving from the god **Thor** + either 'bear' or 'warrior'.

Thorndyke
English – place name; from Old English meaning 'thorn' + 'ditch,
dyke'.

Thornley
English – place name; possibly from several places, but most probably
Thornley in Lancashire, the name deriving from Old English meaning
'thorn' + 'clearing'

Thoroughgood other form of **Thurgood**

Thorpe
Other forms: **Tharp, Thrupp, Thripp**
English – place name; from numerous places, the name deriving from
Old Norse meaning 'hamlet'. Twyla Tharp (1941–) is an American
dancer

Thouless other form of **Thewles**

Thrale
English – occupational; from Old English meaning 'serf'.

Threlfall

English – place name; from a place in Lancashire, the name deriving from Middle English meaning 'serf' + 'clearing'.

Thripp other form of **Thorpe**

Thrupp other form of **Thorpe**

Thurgood

Other forms: **Thoroughgood**, **Thurrowgood**

English – personal name; from the Old Norse god **Thor** + **Geat**, (the name of a tribe), popularly misinterpreted as two familar words 'thorough' and 'good'.

Thurkell other form of **Thurkettle**

Thurkettle

Other forms: **Thirkell**, **Thirkle**, **Thurkell**

English – personal name; from Old Norse meaning **Thor** + 'cauldron' (sacrificial cauldron of the god Thor).

Thurrowgood other form of **Thurgood**

Thynne other form of **Thin**

Tibb

Other forms: **Tebbit**, **Tebboth**, **Tibbett**, **Tibble**, **Tibbott**

English – personal name; from a short form of **Theobald**.

Tickle

Other form: **Tickell**

English – place name; from Tickhill in Yorkshire, the name deriving from Old English meaning 'kid' + 'hill'.

Tiffany

Other forms: **Tiffen**, **Tiffin**

English – personal name; from Greek meaning 'epiphany' or 'showing'. Louis Comfort Tiffany (1848–1933) was an American Art Nouveau glassmaker and interior decorator.

Tigg other form of **Tegg**

Tighe

Other forms: **Tague**, **Teek**

Irish – personal name; anglicized form of Irish Gaelic **Ó Taidhg**, descendant of **Tadhg**, itself meaning 'poet'.

Till, **Tillett** other forms of **Tillott**

Tilley, **Tillie** other forms of **Tilly**

Tilling
English – personal name; either from the familiar form of an Old English male name meaning 'good', or from a familiar form of **Matilda**.

Tillott
Other forms: **Till, Tillett**
English – personal name; from a familiar form of **Matilda**, itself from Norman-French of Germanic origin meaning 'mighty' + 'battle'.

Tilly
Other forms: **Tilley, Tillie**
English
1 personal name; familiar form of **Matilda**.
2 place name; from a place in Shropshire, the name deriving from Old English meaning 'branches, boughs' + 'clearing', or from a place in France, the name deriving from the Latin name **Attilius**.

Timm
Other forms: **Timpson, Tymm**
English – personal name; probably connected with a Germanic name **Timmo**, itself of uncertain origin.

Tindall other form of **Tyndall**

Tippett other form of **Theobald**

Tipple other form of **Theobald**

Tobin
English
1 personal name; from a familiar form of **Tobias**, itself from Hebrew meaning 'God is good'.
2 place name; from St Aubyn, Brittany.

Tod other form of **Todd**

Todd
Other form: **Tod**
Scottish and English – nickname; from Middle English meaning 'fox', referring to someone who in some way resembled the animal.

Tollemache
Other form: **Tammage**
English – occupational; from Old French meaning 'knapsack', referring to a travelling salesman or merchant.

Tolson other form of **Towle**

Tomkin other form of **Thomas**

Tomkiss other form of **Thomas**

Tomlin other form of **Thomas**

Tomlinson other form of **Thomas**

Tonkin other form of **Thomas**

Tonks other form of **Thomas**

Tooke
Other form: **Tuck**
English – personal name; from an Old Norse name **Toki**, itself of uncertain origin.

Tooley other form of **Towle**

Toothill
Other forms: **Tootle**, **Tothill**, **Tottle**
English – place name; from many places, the name deriving from Old English meaning 'lookout' + 'hill'.

Torry other form of **Terry**

Tothill other form of **Toothill**

Tottle other form of **Toothill**

Tovey
English – personal name; from a diminutive form of an Old Norse name **Tofi**, itself meaning 'nation' + 'ruler'.

Towell other form of **Towle**

Towle
Other forms: **Tolson**, **Tooley**, **Towell**
English – personal name; from the Middle English name **Toll**, itself from an Old Norse short form of **Thor** + 'relic'.

Tozer
English – occupational; from Old English meaning 'teaser', a person who combs wool with teasels.

Tranter
English – occupational; from Old French meaning 'carrier, waggoner'.

Travers
Other forms: **Traves**, **Travis**
English – place name/ occupational; from Middle English meaning 'passage, crossing', referring to such a place, or to a toll keeper on a bridge.

Traylor
Other form: **Trayler**
English – occupational; of uncertain origin, possibly from Old French or Old English meaning 'huntsman, tracker', or 'footpad'.

Trelawney
Cornish – place name; from a place in Cornwall, the first part of the name deriving from Cornish meaning 'homestead', the second part of unknown origin.

Tremain
Other form: **Tremayne**
Cornish – place name; from several places in Cornwall, the name deriving from Cornish meaning 'homestead' + 'stone'.

Trevelyan
Cornish – place name; from a place in Cornwall, the name deriving from Cornish meaning 'homestead' + 'mill'. George Macaulay Trevelyan (1876–1962) was an English historian.

Trinder
English – occupational; from Middle English meaning 'to twist', referring to a braider or spinner.

Trollope
English – place name; from an old form of Troughburn in Northumberland, the name deriving from Old Norse meaning 'troll' + Old English meaning 'valley'. Anthony Trollope (1815–82) was an English novelist.

Trumper
English – occupational; from Old French meaning 'trumpeter'.

Truscott
Cornish – place name; from a place in Cornwall, the name deriving from Cornish meaning 'beyond' + 'wood'.

Tuck other form of **Tooke**

Tucker
English – occupational; from Old English meaning 'a person who processed cloth by beating and compressing it'.

Tudball other form of **Theobald**

Tudor
Welsh – personal name; Welsh form of **Theodore**, itself from Greek meaning 'God's gift'. It became a royal surname after the accession of Henry Vll (1457–1509).

Turnbull
N English and Scottish – nickname; for someone who could turn a bull in its course; an old legend claims that the first bearer rescued King Robert the Bruce in this way. But the name may possibly come from Old English meaning 'very bold' or from the Norman-French name **de Trembley**.

Turner
English and Scottish
1 occupational; either from Norman-French of Germanic origin meaning 'to turn on a lathe', referring to a maker of objects on a lathe, or from Old French meaning 'to turn', referring to a person in charge of a tournament.
2 nickname; from Middle English meaning 'to turn', referring to a fast runner.

Tymm other form of **Timm**

Tyndale other form of **Tyndall**

Tyndall
Other forms: **Tindall**, **Tyndale**,
English – place name; from a place in Cumberland, the name deriving from the name of the River Tyne + Old English meaning 'valley, dale'.

Tyson
English – nickname; from Old French meaning 'firebrand'.

u

Udall

English – place name; from Yewdale in Lancashire, the name deriving from Old English meaning 'yew tree' + 'valley'.

Ulman

English – occupational; from Old French meaning 'oil' + Old English meaning 'man', referring to a seller of oil.

Unsworth

English – place name; from a place in Greater Manchester, the name deriving from an Old English name **Hund** (meaning 'dog') + 'enclosure'.

Unwin

English

1 personal name; from an Old English name **Hunwine**, meaning 'bearcub' + 'friend'.

2 nickname; from the Old English negative prefix 'un' + 'friend', referring to an enemy.

Upcott

English – place name; from a place in Devon, the name deriving from Old English meaning 'upper' + 'cottage'.

Upjohn

Welsh – personal name; from Welsh 'ap' meaning 'son of' + **John.**

Upsall

English – place name; from two places in Yorkshire, the name deriving from Old Norse meaning 'upper' + 'hall, dwelling'.

Upton

English – place name; from numerous places, the name deriving from Old English meaning 'upper' + 'settlement'.

Urban

English – personal name; from a medieval name, itself from Latin meaning 'citizen'.

Uren

Cornish – personal name; from Cornish meaning 'born in a town'.

Urmston

English – place name; from a place in Greater Manchester, the name deriving from an Old Norse name meaning 'dragon' + Old English meaning 'settlement'.

Urquhart

Scottish – [in Scotland usually pronounced **ur**-khart] place name; from the lands on Loch Ness, the name deriving from Old Welsh meaning 'on' + 'wood'.

Urwin other form of **Irvine**

Usborne other form of **Osborne**

Usher

English – occupational; from Old English meaning 'door-keeper'.

Usherwood other form of **Isherwood**

Utley

English – place name; from a place in Yorkshire, the name deriving from an Old English name **Utta** + 'clearing'.

V

Vaisey
Other forms: **Feasey, Pheasey, Veasey, Voysey,**
English – nickname; from Norman-French of Germanic origin
meaning 'cheerful, playful', referring to a jolly character.

Vale
English
1 place name; from Old French meaning 'valley'.
2 nickname; other form of **Veale**.

Valrow, Varrow other forms of **Farrar**

Vance other form of **Fenn**

Vann other form of **Fenn**

Varah other form of **Farrar**

Varden other form of **Verden**

Varley
English – place name; from a place in Picardy, France, the name
probably deriving from a Latin name **Virilius**, itself meaning 'manly'.

Vassall
Other form: **Vassar**
English – occupational; from Old French meaning '**servant**'.

Vaughan
1 Welsh – nickname; diminutive form of **Baugh**, itself from Welsh
meaning 'dear'.
2 Irish – personal name; anglicized form of Irish Gaelic **Ó Mócháin** or
Ó Beacháin, the former possibly meaning 'early'.

Veale
English – nickname; from Old French meaning either 'cow or calf' or
'old'. It is often pronounced like **Vale** and its origins have been
confused with those of that name.

Veasey other form of **Vaisey**

Veitch
Scottish – nickname; of uncertain origin. Early forms suggest some
connection with Latin or French meaning 'cow'.

Velden other form of **Field**

Vellacott

English – place name; from a place in Devon, the name probably deriving from Old French meaning 'cow, calf' + Old English meaning 'cottage'.

Venables

English – place name; from a place in France, the name deriving from Latin meaning 'hunting ground'.

Venn other form of **Fenn**

Venton other form of **Fenton**

Ventress other form of **Ventris**

Ventris

Other form: **Ventress**

English – nickname; from Old French meaning 'adventurous'.

Verden

Other forms: **Varden**, **Verdin**, **Verdon**

place name; from a place in France, the name deriving either from Celtic meaning 'hill fort', or else 'alder tree'. See also **Verney** and **Vernon**.

Vernay other form of **Verney**

Verney

Other form: **Vernay**

English – place name; from places in Normandy, the name deriving from Celtic meaning 'alder tree'.

Vernon

English – place name; from a place in Normandy, the name deriving from Celtic meaning 'alder tree'.

Vicar

Other forms: **Vickar**, **Vickers**

English – occupational; from Middle English meaning 'substitute, vicar', originally referring to a parish priest who carried out duties in place of a rector who officially held the benefice or parish church and the entitlement to tithes.

Vidler

English – nickname; from Old French meaning 'face' + 'wolf'.

Viggers
English – nickname; from Middle English meaning 'lusty', referring to a strong, hearty person.

Villiers
English – place name; from many places in France, the name deriving from Latin meaning 'outlying farm or settlement'.

Vincent
Other forms: **Vinsett, Vinson**
English – personal name; from Latin meaning 'conquering'.

Vine
English – place name; from Old French meaning 'vineyard'.

Vinsett other form **Vincent**

Vinson other form of **Vincent**

Vokes, Volkes, Volks other forms of **Foulkes**

Voller other forms of **Fuller**

Voysey other form of **Vaisey**

W

Waddell
Other form: **Waddle**
Scottish – [in Scotland usually pronounced 'woddle'] place
name; from an old name (Wedale) for Stow in Midlothian, possibly
deriving from Old English meaning 'look-out hill'.

Waddilove other form of **Waddilow**

Waddilow
Other form: **Waddilove**
English – personal name; from an Old English name **Wealdtheof**,
itself meaning 'power' + 'thief'.

Waddington
English – place name; from various places, the name deriving from an
Old English name **Wada** + 'settlement'.

Waddle other form of **Waddell**

Wade
English – personal name; from an Old English name of a mythical sea
giant **Wada**, itself from Old English meaning 'to go'.

Wadsworth
Other form: **Wordsworth**
English – place name; from a place in Yorkshire, the name deriving
from an Old English name **Wada** (see **Wade**) + 'enclosure'. William
Wordsworth (1770–1850) was an English poet.

Wagstaff
English – occupational; from Middle English meaning 'to brandish' +
'staff', referring to an official who carried a staff of office.

Wain
English – Other form: **Wayne**
occupational; from Middle English meaning 'cart', referring to a
maker of carts.

Wainwright
English – occupational; from Middle English meaning 'maker of
carts'.

Waite
English – occupational; from Norman-French of Germanic origin meaning 'watch, watchman'. Terry Waite (1939–) is an English religious adviser who was taken hostage while on a mission in Beirut.

Wakeham
English – place name; from places in Devon and Sussex, the name deriving from an Old English name **Waca** meaning 'watchful' + 'homestead'.

Wakelin
English – personal name; diminutive form of a Norman-French name of Germanic origin.

Walbrook
English – place name; from a place in London, the name deriving from Old English meaning 'Welsh person, foreigner' + 'brook'.

Walcott
English – place name; from places in many counties, the name deriving from Old English meaning 'Welsh person, foreigner' + 'cottage'.

Walden
English – place name; from many places, the name deriving from Old English meaning 'Welsh person, foreigner' + 'valley'.

Walderne other form of **Waldron**

Walding, **Waldman** other forms of **Weald**

Waldron
Other form: **Walderne**
English – place name; from Old English meaning 'wood' + 'house'.

Walker
English and Scottish
1 occupational; from Middle English meaning 'a fuller of cloth' (see **Fuller**).
2 place name; from a place in Northumberland, the name deriving from Middle English meaning 'wall', referring to the Roman wall, + 'marsh'.

Wall
English – place name; from Old English meaning 'wall', referring to a place which has a Roman wall or a sea wall.

Wallace
Other form: **Wallis**
Scottish, Irish and English – nickname; from Norman-French of

Germanic origin, meaning 'foreign', referring to various people of Celtic origin, e.g. Welsh, Bretons, in Scotland probably to the Britons of Strathclyde (now SW Scotland). Sir William Wallace (1274–1305) was a Scottish patriot in the Wars of Independence against England.

Walley [pronounced '**wall**-ee']

Other form: **Whalley**

English – place name; from places in Lancashire and Cheshire, the name deriving from Old English meaning 'hill' + 'wood, clearing'.

Wallis other form of Wallace

Walmer

English – place name; from places in Kent and Lancashire, the name deriving from Old English meaning either 'wood' + 'bog', or 'Welsh' + 'pool'.

Walpole

English – place name; from places in Norfolk and Suffolk, the name deriving from Old English meaning 'wall' + 'pool'.

Walsh

Other forms: **Welsh**, **Welch**

1 English – nickname; from Middle English meaning 'foreign', referring to a Celt.

2 Irish – personal name; anglicized form of the Irish Gaelic name **Breatnach**, itself from Irish Gaelic meaning 'British, Welsh'.

Walter

English – personal name; from Germanic meaning 'rule' + 'army'.

Ward

1 English – occupational; from Old English meaning 'guard, watchman'.

2 Irish – personal name; anglicized form of Irish Gaelic **Mac an Bhaird**, itself meaning 'son of the bard'.

Ware

English – place name; from a place in Hertfordshire, the name deriving from Old English meaning 'weir, dam'.

Wark

English – place name; from places in Northumberland, the name deriving from Old English meaning 'building works'.

Warlock other form of Werlock

Warne

English – nickname; from Old English meaning 'eager, zealous'.

Warner

English – personal name; from a Norman-French personal name of Germanic origin, itself meaning 'army of **Warin**'. Warner Brothers, founded by Jack, Harry and Samuel Warner in the 1920s, became a major American film studio of the 20th century

Warren

English – place name; from a place in France, the name deriving from Norman-French meaning 'game park'.

Wassall, **Wassell** other forms of **Wastell**

Wastell

Other forms: **Wassall**, **Wassell**

English

1 occupational; from Norman-French of Germanic origin meaning 'cake', referring to a baker of fancy bread and cake,

2 place name; from a place in Worcestershire, the name deriving from Old English meaning 'guardhouse'.

Watkin, **Watkins**, **Watkinson** other forms of **Watt**

Watmore other form of **Watmough** or **Whatmore**

Watmough

Other forms: **Watmore**, **Watmuff**

English – personal name; from the Middle English name **Watt**, itself a familiar form of **Walter** + a term from Middle English meaning 'related by marriage'. See also **Watt.**

Watson other form of **Watt**

Watt

Other forms: **Watkin(s)**, **Watkinson**, **Watson**, **Watts**

English and Scottish – personal name; from the Middle English name **Watt**, a familiar form of **Walter**,

Wavell

English – place name; from a place in France, the name deriving from Old French meaning 'valley' + 'settlement'.

Wayne other form of **Wain**

Weald

Other forms: **Walding**, **Waldman**, **Weld**, **Wold**

English – place name; from Old English meaning 'forest', though after

widespread forest clearances, it came to refer to uncultivated upland
areas formerly forested.

Weatherall

Other forms: **Wederell**, **Weatherill**

English – place name; from a place in Cumbria, the name deriving
from Old English meaning 'ram' + 'nook, recess'.

Webb

Other forms: **Webber**, **Webster**

English – occupational; from Middle English meaning 'weaver'.
Sidney (1859–1947) and Beatrice (1858–1943) Webb, were social
reformers, historians and economists.

Wedderburn

Scottish – place name; from a place in Berwickshire, the name deriving
from Old English meaning 'wether' (castrated male sheep) + 'stream'.

Wederell other form of **Weatherall**

Weekes other form of **Wick**

Welch other form of **Walsh**

Weld other form of **Weald**

Weldon

English – place name; from a place in Northhamptonshire, the name
deriving from Old English meaning 'spring' + 'hill'.

Welsh other form of **Walsh**

Wensley

English – place name; from places in Derbyshire and Yorkshire, the
former deriving from the Old English name of **Woden** (the god) +
'grove, clearing', the latter from Old English meaning 'Vandals' (the
tribe) + 'grove, clearing'.

Wentworth

English – place name; from places in Cambridgeshire and Yorkshire,
the name deriving either from an Old English name **Wintra** +
'enclosure' or from Old English meaning 'winter enclosure', referring
to somewhere inhabited only in winter.

Werlock

Other form: **Warlock**

English – nickname; from Old English meaning 'wizard'.

Whalley other form of **Walley**

Wharfe

English – place name; from a place in Yorkshire, the name deriving from Old Norse meaning 'nook, corner', or else from Old English meaning 'wharfe, embankment', as in the case of the River Wharfe.

Whatley other form of **Wheatley**

Whatmore

Other form: **Watmore**

English – place name; from a place in Shropshire, the name deriving from Old English meaning 'damp' or 'bend' + 'moor'.

Wheatcroft

English – place name; from several places, the name deriving from Old English meaning 'wheat' + 'smallholding'.

Wheatley

Other form: **Whatley**

English – place name; from many places, the name deriving from Old English meaning 'wheat' + 'clearing'.

Whitaker

English – place name; from many places, the name deriving from Old English meaning 'white' or 'wheat' + 'cultivated land'.

Whitbread

English – occupational; from Old English meaning 'white' or 'wheat' + 'bread', referring to a baker.

Whitehorn

English – place name; from Old English meaning 'white' + 'house'.

Whitelaw

Scottish and N English – place name; from several places of this name in S Scotland and N England, the name deriving from Old English meaning 'white' + 'hill'.

Whitney

English – place name; from a place in Herefordshire, the first part of the name probably deriving from Old English meaning 'white' and the second meaning 'island'.

Whittle

English – place name; from places in Lancashire and Northumberland, the name deriving from Old English meaning 'white' + 'hill'.

Wick
Other forms: **Weekes, Wick(es), Wix**
English – place name; from Old English meaning 'hamlet' or 'dairy farm'.

Widdowson
English – nickname; from Old English meaning 'son of the widow'.

Widlake
English – place name; from a place in Devon, the name deriving from Old English meaning 'wide' + 'stream'.

Wigg
English – nickname; probably from Old English meaning 'beetle'.

Wilberforce
Other form: **Wilberfoss**
English – place name; from a place in Humberside, the name deriving from an Old English personal name **Wilburh** (meaning 'will' + 'fortress') + Old English meaning 'ditch'. William Wilberforce (1759–1833) was an English politician and philanthropist who campaigned against the slave trade until it was abolished in 1807.

Wilkie
Scottish – personal name; from a familiar form of **William**. Sir David Wilkie (1785–1841) was a well-known Scottish painter.

Wilkin
Other form: **Wilkins, Wilkinson**
English – personal name; from a medieval name, itself a familiar form of **William.**

Will
Other forms: **Willett, Willis, Wilson**
Scottish and English – personal name; from a medieval name **Will**, itself a familiar form of **William.** Harold Wilson (1916–95) was a British prime minister.

William
Other forms: **Fitzwilliam, Gilham, Gill(i)am, Wilmott, Williams, Williamson, Willett**
English – personal name; from Norman-French of Germanic origin meaning 'will' + 'protection'.

Willis other form of **Will**

Willoughby
English – place name; from many places, the name deriving from Old English meaning 'willow' + Old Norse meaning 'settlement'.

Wilmott other form of **William**

Wilson other form of **Will**

Windsor
English – place name; from places in Berkshire and Dorset, the name deriving from Old English meaning 'windlass' + 'bank', referring to a place for hauling up boats. Since 1917, it has been the surname of the British royal family.

Winslow
English – place name; from a place in Buckinghamshire, the name deriving from Old English meaning 'friend' + 'mound, barrow'.

Winterbottom
English – place name; from a place in Cheshire, the name deriving from Middle English meaning 'winter' + 'valley', referring to a place where someone had his main house in winter, his summer residence being in temporary pastures elsewhere.

Wishart
Scottish – personal name; from the Norman-French name **Guiscard**, itself deriving from Old French meaning 'wise' + 'bold'.

Witherspoon other form of **Wotherspoon**

Withnell
English – place name; from a place in Lancashire, the name deriving from Old English meaning 'willows' + 'hill'.

Wix other form of **Wick**

Wogan
Welsh – personal name; from an Old Welsh name **Gwygan**, meaning 'little scowler'. The surname was transferred to Ireland where it is common now.

Wold other form of **Weald**

Wolseley other form of **Wolsey**

Wolsey
Other form: **Wolseley**
English – personal name; from an Old English name **Wulfsige**, itself meaning 'wolf' + 'victory'.

Wood
Other form: **Woods**
English
1 place name; from Old English meaning 'wood, forest'.
2 nickname; from Old English meaning 'mad, distracted'.

Woodruff
Other form: **Woodrup**
English – nickname; from Old English meaning 'woodruff' (a scented herb), referring to someone who used perfumes.

Woods other form of **Wood**

Woodward
English – occupational; from Old English meaning 'forester, keeper of the woods'.

Woolley
English – place name; from many places, the name deriving from Old English meaning 'wolves' + 'wood'.

Woolrich other form of **Woolridge**

Woolridge
Other form: **Woolrich**
English – personal name; from an Old English name **Wulfric**, itself meaning 'wolf' + 'power'.

Wootton
English – place name; from numerous places, the name deriving from Old English meaning 'wood, clearing' + 'settlement'.

Wordsworth other form of **Wadsworth**

Wotherspoon
Other form: **Witherspoon**
Scottish – place name; of doubtful origin, possibly deriving from Old English meaning 'sheep' + 'piece of land'. Rev John Witherspoon (1723–94) played an active part in the American War of Independence.

Wray other form of **Ray**

Wright
Other form: **Wrightson**
English – occupational; from Old English meaning 'craftsman, maker'. The Wright brothers, Orville (1871–1948) and Wilbur (1867–1912), were pioneers of flying.and founded an aircraft production company.

Wrigley
English – place name; from a place near Manchester, the name
deriving from Old English. The first element is of unknown meaning,
the second means 'clearing, field'.

Y

Yardley
Other form: **Yeardley**
English – place name; from many places, the name deriving from Old English meaning 'pole, stick' + 'wood'.

Yarwood
English – place name; the second element deriving from Old English meaning 'wood', the first being of uncertain origin. Suggestions include Old English meaning 'eagle' or 'fish trap'.

Yate other form of **Yates**

Yates
Other forms: **Yate**, **Yeates**, **Yeats**
English – place name; from a place in Gloucestershire, the name deriving from Old English meaning 'gate, gap'.

Yeardley other form of **Yardley**

Yearsley
English – place name; from a place in Yorkshire, the name deriving from Old English meaning 'boar' + 'wood'.

Yeates, **Yeats** other form of **Yates**

Yeo [pronounced yo]
English – place name; from numerous places in Devon and Cornwall, the name deriving from SW English dialect meaning 'river'.

Yong, Yonge other forms of **Young**

Young
Other forms: **Yong**, **Yonge**, **Younger**
English – nickname; from Old English meaning 'junior', referring to a younger brother or a son.

Younghusband
English – occupational; from Old English meaning 'young farmer'.

Yule
Other form: **Yuill**
Scottish – nickname; for a person born on Christmas Day, from the old word for Christmas time and for its preceding pagan festival.

Z

Zebedee
English – personal name; from Hebrew meaning 'gift of God'.

Zouch
Other form: **Such, Sutch**
English – place name; probably from a place in France, the name deriving from Old French meaning 'tree stump'. In the Middle Ages, the Leicestershire town of Ashby de la Zouch was owned by Roger de la Zuche.